count on us...™

COUNTING YOUR FAT

COUNTING YOUR CALORIES

SALT BALANCED

inspirational recipes for good health

THE NEW COLLECTION

Adam Palmer

MARKS & SPENCER

Marks and Spencer plc

PO Box 3339, Chester CH99 9QS

www.marksandspencer.com

Created and produced by The Bridgewater Book Company Ltd.

Marks and Spencer would like to thank Adam Palmer for the recipes in this book and for his contribution to the introduction. They would also like to thank Fiona Hunter for her contribution to the introduction and for her work as consultant nutritionist and Fiona Moore and Jenny Arthur for their help in the making of this book.

Marks and Spencer would also like to thank Karen Thomas (photographer), Valerie Berry (home economist), Breda Bradshaw (home economist) and Charlie Parker (marketing nutritionist).

ISBN: 1-84461-060-8

Printed in China

NOTES

V

This symbol means the recipe is suitable for vegetarians.

This book uses both metric and imperial measurements. Follow the same unit of measurement throughout; do not mix metric and imperial.

All spoon measurements are level unless otherwise specified.

Recipes using raw or very lightly cooked eggs should be avoided by infants, the elderly, pregnant women, convalescents, and anyone suffering from an illness.

The times given are an approximate guide only. Preparation times differ according to the techniques used by different people and the cooking times may also vary from those given. Optional ingredients, variations or serving suggestions have not been included in the calculations.

DISCLAIMER

Before following any of the advice given in this book we recommend that you first check with your doctor. Pregnant women, women planning to become pregnant, children, diabetics or people with other medical conditions should always check with their doctor or health care professional before embarking on any type of diet. This book is not intended as a substitute for your doctor's or dietician's advice and support, but should complement the advice they give you. The accuracy of the nutritional information (calorie, fat and salt) given for each recipe is dependent on following the recipe instructions.

The views expressed in this book are those of the author but they are general views only and readers are urged to consult a relevant and qualified specialist for individual advice in particular situations. Marks and Spencer p.l.c. and Exclusive Editions Limited hereby exclude all liability to the extent permitted by law for any errors or omissions in this book and for any loss, damage or expense (whether direct or indirect) suffered by a third party relying on any information contained in this book.

CONTENTS

introduction

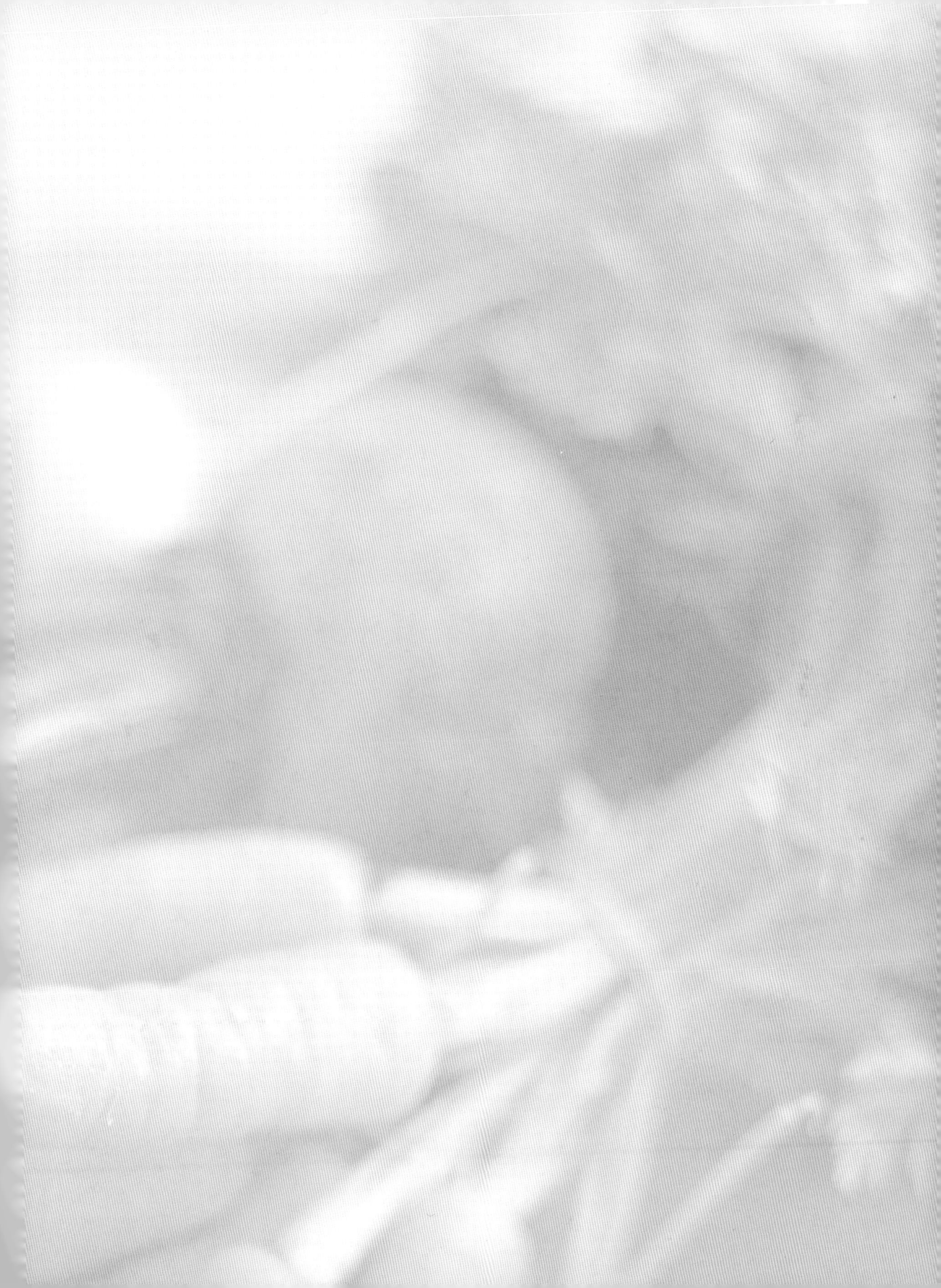

EAT YOURSELF HEALTHY

Healthy eating and weight loss do not rely simply on eating less food. A fitter, trimmer body requires certain changes in the way we prepare and cook our everyday food and when we eat it. There are hundreds of different diet plans for us to try – some of which are specific to one or two particular food groups and do not concentrate on adopting a varied and balanced approach to healthy eating. Food plays an important role in our well-being and with the hectic pace of modern life it is often much easier to skip meals and grab food 'on the hoof' and snack throughout the day on highly processed foods which depend too much on fat, salt and sugar for any flavour – all which we now know to be particularly detrimental, not only to our waistlines but also to our long-term health if consumed in quantity. The recipes in this new **count on us...** collection serve to demonstrate how you can lighten up your cooking by using less fat, salt and sugar and instead draw on the natural flavours in foods, without any compromise on taste.
The use of vegetable oil sprays, cooking with non-stick cookware and using silicone sheets in your oven trays enables you to brown and caramelise meats, fish and vegetables in the oven or under the grill without having to use excessive amounts of added fat. Foods naturally contain salt so you should not add extra salt during cooking but find alternative ways of boosting flavour. The recipes in this book include no added

salt, relying instead on the additions of fresh herbs, spices and citrus juice to enhance the taste experience of the finished dish.

By following the recipes in this new collection you will be able to complement the 220 or so dishes already available in the **count on us...** range. What could be better than a home-cooked meal prepared for your family and friends with the added advantage of being less than 3% fat, calorie-controlled and low in salt and sugar?

We hope that the recipes will not only change your waistline but also the way you cook and enjoy your food.

Happy healthy cooking!

Adam Palmer

Adam Palmer, one of the UK's top chefs, is renowned for his healthy and innovative cuisine. He has developed the delicious recipes you will enjoy in this book. A former Executive Chef at Champney's Health Resort, Adam is a pioneer of delicious alternatives to outdated dietary practices and is involved with developing further dishes in the **count on us...** *range. He is the author of two other cookery titles, has created recipes for many leading magazines in the UK, Europe and the USA, and is a regular guest on TV cookery programmes.*

THE 3 MAIN REASONS THAT DIETS FAIL

Setting unrealistic goals – if you set unrealistic goals you're more likely to become disheartened and give up. Aim for a slow but steady weight loss of 0.5–1kg (1–2lb) a week. If you lose too much weight too quickly there's a danger of losing lean muscle tissue as well as fat.

Following the wrong sort of diet – however tempting they may seem, crash diets just don't work. Although you may lose weight initially, you'll find you'll end up putting on not just the weight you originally lost but more.

Not eating enough – a mistake people often make is to reduce their calorie intake too heavily. Overly strict diets are difficult to stick to in the long run, they're not necessary and they're not healthy. If you restrict your calories too severely the chances are you'll end up missing out on important nutrients.

HOW TO USE YOUR COUNT ON US... COOKBOOK

Losing weight isn't always easy, but the benefits are enormous – you'll feel fitter and more confident, you'll have more energy and you'll be healthier. The good news is that losing weight doesn't mean having to say goodbye to your favourite foods; in fact it's important to include the foods you enjoy eating. A diet which leaves you feeling deprived, unhappy and dissatisfied is a diet that's very quickly going to be abandoned.

With increasing pressure on our daily schedule many of us don't always have the time to cook meals from scratch, which is why Marks and Spencer have developed the **count on us...** range. **count on us...** has been developed for people who love their food but want to lose a little weight. All the products in the range are less than 3% fat, calorie-controlled and low in salt.

The range has been designed to provide a nutritionally balanced eating plan for women with a target intake of around 1400 calories a day and for men of around 2000 calories a day. The aim is to help people achieve gradual but steady and sustained weight loss.

Breakfast

Lunch

Main meal

Dessert

There are now some 220 products in the range – with choices for most eating occasions. Following a diet can be very boring if you have to eat the same foods day after day so we're continually developing new products to include favourite dishes, which would normally be forbidden in most diets.

The recipes in this book are intended to complement the **count on us...** range; each recipe comes with a nutritional breakdown of the calorie, total fat, saturated fat and salt content.

A BALANCED APPROACH TO HEALTHY EATING

The food we eat can have an important and lasting effect on our health. Our body needs over 40 different nutrients to stay healthy. Some, such as carbohydrates, proteins and fats, are required in relatively large quantities, while others, such as vitamins, minerals and trace elements, are required in only minute amounts but are no less essential for health.

The best way to ensure that we get the full range of all the nutrients our bodies need is to eat a varied diet containing foods from each of the 5 food groups. The secret to healthy eating and managing your weight is to get the balance right.

BALANCE OF GOOD HEALTH

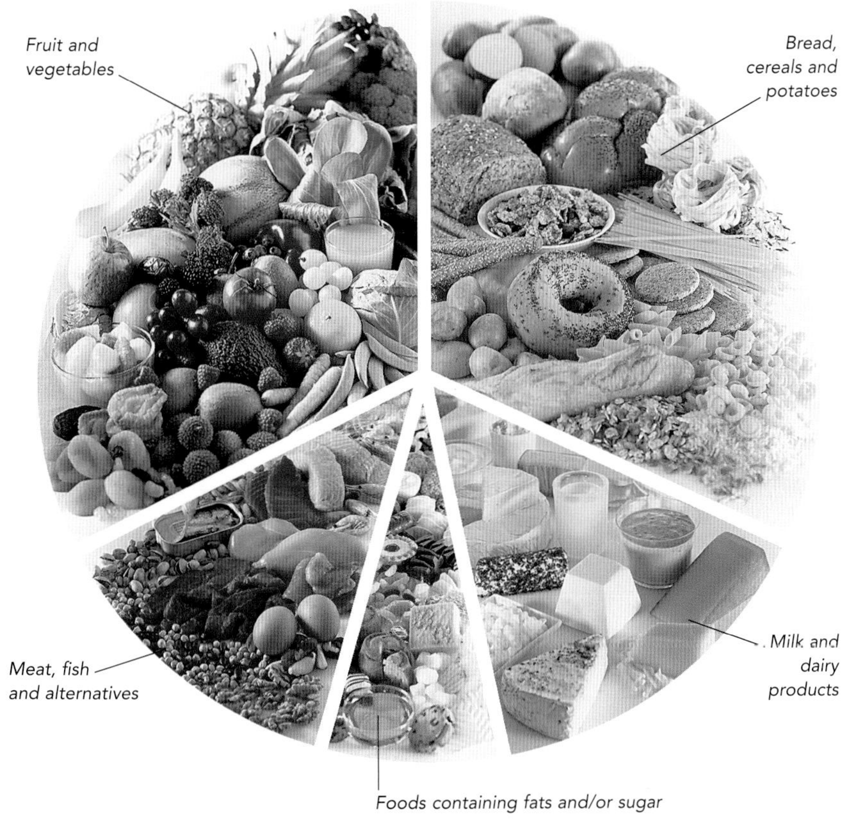

Based on the Balance of Good Health with kind permission of the Food Standards Agency

BREAD, CEREALS AND POTATOES (E.G. BREAD, RICE, PASTA, NOODLES, BREAKFAST CEREALS) – KNOWN AS COMPLEX OR STARCHY CARBOHYDRATES

Foods from this group should provide around one-third of your calories each day. These foods provide carbohydrates, dietary fibre, protein, vitamins and minerals but their main job is to provide energy.

Choose fibre-rich varieties such as wholemeal bread and wholegrain cereals – they provide slow-release energy which helps keep blood sugar levels stable.

Contrary to what many people believe, foods from this group are not fattening in themselves, becoming highly calorific only when eaten with lots of fat (a rich, creamy sauce with pasta, fried potatoes, or bread spread thickly with butter).

• Eat at least 5 servings from this group each day.

1 serving equals:

3tbsp breakfast cereal

1 slice bread

2 heaped tbsp boiled rice

3 heaped tbsp pasta

2 egg-sized potatoes

FRUIT AND VEGETABLES

It's no coincidence that people from Mediterranean countries who eat almost twice the amount of fruit and vegetables we do live longer and remain healthier. Fruit and vegetables provide vitamins and minerals, dietary fibre and phytochemicals, which may help protect against diseases such as cancer and heart disease.

The advice from experts is that we should all aim to eat at least 5 portions of fruit and vegetables a day. This has been proved to help prevent a number of diseases including heart disease and several forms of cancer.

Apart from being excellent providers of vitamins and minerals, most fruit and vegetables are fat-free and wonderfully low in calories. Make the most of them and look out for new recipes and ideas for cooking them – try poaching, baking or grilling fruits as an alternative to eating them raw.

- Aim to eat at least 5 portions of fruit and vegetables a day.
- Adopt a rainbow approach – different-coloured fruit and vegetables provide different vitamins and minerals.
- Frozen, canned and dried fruits and vegetables as well as juices are all useful in helping you reach your daily target.

1 serving equals 80g (3oz) of fruit or vegetables, a total of 400g (14oz) per day:

Fresh

1 small glass (150ml/5fl oz) unsweetened fruit juice

1 slice melon or pineapple

1 apple, orange, peach or pear

Frozen

80g (3oz) frozen peas, sweetcorn or berries

Dried

1 x 15ml sp (1tbsp) dried fruit e.g. raisins

Canned

3 x 15ml sp (3tbsp) fruit salad or canned fruit or vegetables

MILK AND DAIRY PRODUCTS (E.G. MILK, YOGHURT, CHEESE) – THIS GROUP DOES NOT INCLUDE BUTTER, EGGS AND CREAM

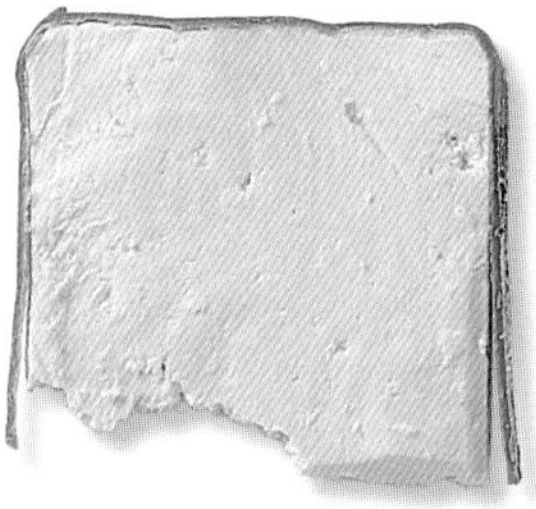

Dairy products are an important source of calcium, essential for strong bones and teeth. Many people, especially teenage girls, fail to eat enough calcium to meet their recommended daily requirement – putting them at risk of the bone disease osteoporosis in later life. As many as 1 in 3 women and 1 in 12 men over the age of 50 in the UK suffer from osteoporosis.

Dairy foods also provide protein, vitamin A, phosphorus, vitamin D and vitamin B_2. Foods in this group can be high in fat, particularly saturated fat – choose reduced-fat and low-fat alternatives such as skimmed and semi-skimmed milk. Calcium is contained in the non-creamy portion of milk so when the fat is removed to make reduced-fat products the calcium remains – in fact, pint for pint, skimmed milk contains slightly more calcium than whole milk.

- Aim to eat 2–3 servings from this group a day.
- Choose low- and reduced-fat varieties whenever possible.

1 serving equals:
1 glass milk (200ml/⅓pint)
150g (5oz) yoghurt
100g (3½oz) cottage cheese
40g (1½oz) hard full-fat cheese e.g. Cheddar

MEAT, FISH AND ALTERNATIVES (POULTRY, EGGS, BEANS AND PULSES, NUTS AND SEEDS)

Foods from this group provide protein, needed for the production of enzymes, antibodies and hormones – in short, protein is vital to ensure our bodies function properly. In the UK, we commonly have plenty of protein in our diet. Foods in this group are also a good source of iron, needed by the blood to circulate oxygen around the body. As many as 1 in 3 women in the UK have been found to have low iron stores, which causes tiredness, lethargy and possibly anaemia.

- Aim to eat 2–4 servings from this group a day.
- Meat should be lean with any visible fat removed before cooking.
- Meat can be fresh, frozen or part of a prepared meal.
- Aim to eat at least 2 servings of fish per week, one of which should be an oil-rich fish such as salmon, mackerel or fresh tuna (canned tuna does not count). All are rich in omega-3 fatty acids, and help to reduce the risk of heart disease.
- Vegetarians should eat a variety of different protein foods to ensure they get all the nutrients they need.

1 serving equals approximately:
90g (3½oz) red meat
125g (4oz) chicken
125–150g (4–5oz) fish
5tbsp baked beans
2tbsp nuts

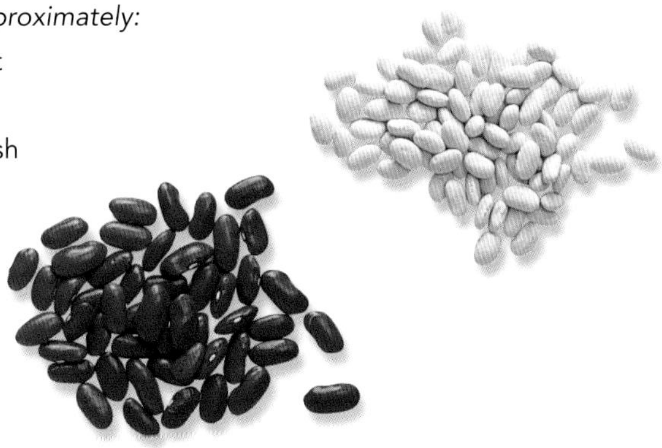

FOODS CONTAINING FATS AND SUGARS

Small amounts of fat are vital in our diet to provide essential fatty acids and to facilitate the absorption of fat-soluble vitamins, but a high-fat diet is known to increase the risk of heart disease, certain types of cancer and obesity. A diet that is rich in saturated fats, found in foods such as fatty cuts of meat and meat products, full-fat dairy products, butter and some types of margarine, increases the levels of cholesterol in the blood.

Weight for weight, fat provides twice as many calories as carbohydrate or protein. There is also some evidence to suggest that calories eaten as fat are more likely to be laid down as body fat than calories from protein or carbohydrate. The good news is that these days low in fat doesn't have to mean low in taste. There are easy ways to trim the fat from your diet (see page 20) without giving up the foods you enjoy.

Sugar provides 'empty' calories – calories that provide nothing else in the way of protein, fibre, vitamins or minerals, and calories that most of us could do without. So it makes sense to cut down on it where you can. Sugar and sugary foods also increase the risk of tooth decay, especially when eaten between meals.

- Total fat should provide no more than 35% of your total calories each day. For a woman eating 2000 calories a day this amounts to 70g (2½oz) of fat.
- Saturated fat should provide no more than 10% of your total fat intake. For a woman eating 2000 calories a day this amounts to 21g (¾oz) of fat.
- Look at the nutrition labelling on food packaging to check the fat content of the food, looking particularly at the amount of saturated fat.
- Avoid adding sugar to food.

DIETARY FIBRE

Although it passes through our digestive tract unchanged, fibre is essential for a healthy digestive system.

Fibre can be divided into two groups: insoluble fibre and soluble fibre. Insoluble fibre is found mainly in wheat, wholegrain cereals, fruit and vegetables and pulses. It has the effect of holding or absorbing water, which helps to prevent constipation and diverticular disease. It also speeds up the rate at which waste material is passed through the body and this is believed to play an important role in preventing bowel cancer by reducing the length of time that cancer-causing toxins stay within the digestive system.

Soluble fibre, found in oats and oat bran, beans and pulses and some fruits, can help to lower high blood cholesterol levels and slow down the absorption of sugar into the bloodstream.

The recommended daily intake of fibre for men and women is 18g (½oz). Surveys show that only 2 out of 10 people reach this target.

EASY WAYS TO INCREASE YOUR FIBRE INTAKE:

- Choose a wholegrain cereal such as porridge, muesli or bran flakes for breakfast. Choose one that provides 3g of fibre or more per serving.
- Choose wholemeal or Granary bread. Just because bread is brown it doesn't necessarily mean that it is high in fibre – look for the words wholegrain, wholewheat or wholemeal on the label.
- Eat more beans and pulses such as lentils, red kidney beans and chickpeas.
- Eat a minimum of 5 servings of fruit and vegetables a day.
- Eat ready-to-eat dried fruit as a between-meals snack or add it to your breakfast cereal.
- Use brown rather than white rice, and wholemeal pasta.

SALT (SODIUM CHLORIDE)

Sodium plays a vital role in the body's fluid balance as well as being involved in muscle and nerve activity. Almost all of us, however, consume far more than is good for us. A high salt intake is believed to be a major factor in the development of high blood pressure, which increases the risk of stroke and heart disease.

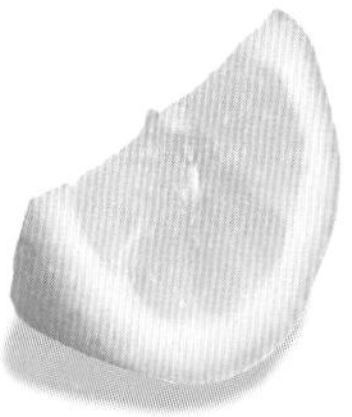

- Experts recommend reducing daily salt intake to no more than 6g (⅙oz) (equivalent to 2.4g sodium). This is only 1 teaspoon of salt, which is around half our current average intake.
- Around 80% of the sodium in our diet comes from processed foods – one small can of chicken soup, for instance, can contain over half the recommended daily amount.
- Train your tastebuds to enjoy foods with less salt. Try using herbs and spices, lemon or mustard to flavour your foods.
- As a general rule, foods that contain more than 0.5g sodium per serving are high in sodium. Foods that contain less than 0.1g sodium per serving are low in sodium. Always read the nutritional labelling on packaging.
- The **count on us...** range has strictly controlled levels of salt.

WATER

Water is vital to good health. Unlike some other nutrients, the human body does not store water so you need to drink a regular supply.

Some foods, particularly fruit and vegetables, contain quite a lot of water – a slice of watermelon, for instance, is 92% water and an apple 84% – and eating them can help replace some of the water lost by the body. We still need to drink around 1.8 litres (3 pints) of fluid, which is the equivalent of 8 to 10 glasses each day, to prevent the body from becoming dehydrated.

Around 85% of our brain tissue is water – which explains why even mild dehydration can lead to problems such as headaches, lethargy, dizziness and an inability to concentrate. Long-term dehydration can lead to digestive problems, kidney problems and joint pain. Relying on thirst to tell you when you need to take a drink is not a good idea – by the time you feel thirsty your body is probably already mildly dehydrated.

- Drink at least 8 to 10 glasses (a glass is about 225ml/8fl oz) of fluid a day.
- Don't rely on thirst as a sign that you need to take a drink.
- Eat plenty of fruit and vegetables to help increase your fluid intake.
- Take water breaks rather than coffee breaks at regular intervals during the day.
- Keeping a bottle of water on your desk at work will remind you to take a drink.
- To check to see you are drinking enough fluid look at your urine – if you're drinking enough it should be a light yellow colour. Dark yellow urine is a sign you're not drinking enough.
- Drink plenty of water before, during and after taking exercise – especially in warm weather.

ALCOHOL

Alcohol is not forbidden on a diet but it is worth remembering that for most of us willpower dissolves in alcohol! A glass of wine may only be 85 calories but the trouble is that one glass easily leads to another and after a couple of drinks it's easy to forget about your good intentions to eat healthily. If you drink alcohol, stay within the recommended safe guidelines which are no more than 2–3 units a day for women, 3–4 units a day for men, with 2–3 alcohol-free days during the week.

1 unit equals:
1 (125ml/4fl oz) glass of wine
300ml (½pint) ordinary-strength beer or cider
1 single measure (25ml/1fl oz) spirits
1 single measure (50ml/2fl oz) port or sherry

8 STEPS TO A HEALTHY DIET
Enjoy your food
Eat a variety of different foods
Eat the right amount to achieve a healthy weight
Eat plenty of foods rich in carbohydrates and fibre
Eat plenty of fruit and vegetables
Don't eat too many foods that contain a lot of fat
Don't have sugary foods and drinks too often
Drink alcohol sensibly

LOSING WEIGHT SAFELY

If you're trying to lose weight you're not alone. 41% of men and 33% of women in the UK are now classified as overweight (BMI over 25 – see page 19), and 25% of men and 20% of women are obese (BMI over 30). The number of obese people in the UK has trebled since 1990. If the current trends continue at least one-third of adults will be classified as obese by 2020. Many nutritionists believe that the reason for this alarming rise is due not to our eating more but to our doing less. Modern technology and labour-saving devices mean that we're much less active than we used to be.

Our weight is a reflection of the balance between the energy (calories) we consume and the energy we use. Our energy intake is determined by the amount and type of food we eat. Our energy expenditure is determined by a combination of our resting metabolic rate and the amount of calories we burn in day-to-day activities.

The resting metabolic rate is the amount of energy our body needs to keep it ticking over, similar to the fuel used by a car when the engine is idling but the car is stationary. If our energy intake equals our energy expenditure our body weight will remain the same, but if our intake exceeds our expenditure the excess energy is stored in the body as fat (see below).

THE SEESAW EFFECT

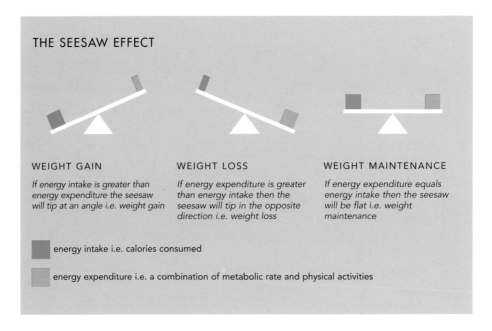

WEIGHT GAIN

If energy intake is greater than energy expenditure the seesaw will tip at an angle i.e. weight gain

WEIGHT LOSS

If energy expenditure is greater than energy intake then the seesaw will tip in the opposite direction i.e. weight loss

WEIGHT MAINTENANCE

If energy expenditure equals energy intake then the seesaw will be flat i.e. weight maintenance

energy intake i.e. calories consumed

energy expenditure i.e. a combination of metabolic rate and physical activities

THE IDEAL RATE OF WEIGHT LOSS

Experts agree the best and safest way to lose weight is slowly and steadily – between 0.5 and 1kg (1 and 2lb) a week is the ideal rate. If you lose too much weight too quickly there is a danger of losing lean muscle tissue as well as fat. Since our basal metabolic rate (the number of calories the body needs to function) is related to the amount of lean muscle tissue we have it's a good idea to do whatever we can to preserve it.

HOW LOW SHOULD YOU GO?

The total number of calories we need to eat each day varies depending on a number of factors such as age, weight, sex, activity levels, body composition and metabolic rate. As a general guide, women need around 2000 calories a day and men need 2500. To lose 0.5kg (1lb) a week, you need to reduce your calorie intake by 500 calories a day. Diets that restrict calories too severely (fewer than 1000 calories a day for women) are not recommended.

HOW YOU SHAPE UP

Although most of us can get a pretty good idea of whether we need to lose weight or not just by looking in the mirror, if you want a more accurate assessment you can calculate your body mass index or waist circumference (see panel below).

HOW YOU SHAPE UP

BMI (Body Mass Index) = your weight (in kilograms) ÷ your height (in metres) squared.
For example:

$$\frac{60\text{kg}}{(1.65\text{m} \times 1.65\text{m})} = \mathbf{22}$$

1kg = 2.2lb 1m = 39.37in

Under 18.5	*underweight*
19–24.9	*healthy weight range*
25–29.9	*overweight*
30–40	*obese*
Over 40	*severely obese*

WAIST CIRCUMFERENCE

Men

Waist circumference over 94cm (37in) *indicates a slight health risk*

Waist circumference over 102cm (40in) *indicates a substantial health risk*

Women

Waist circumference over 80cm (32in) *indicates a slight health risk*

Waist circumference over 88cm (35in) *indicates a substantial health risk*

TRIMMING THE FAT

Fat provides twice as many calories as either protein or carbohydrate, which is why the most effective way of reducing calories is to limit the amount of fat you use.

- Start with low-fat ingredients – white fish, shellfish, chicken and lean meat are all good choices.
- Trim off visible fat from meat before cooking and remove the skin from poultry. Avoid red meat that has too much fat or marbling.
- Choose low-fat cooking techniques – poach, braise, steam, roast, grill or stir-fry. Marinades are a good way of adding extra flavour without fat.
- Invest in a good heavy-based non-stick pan and remember that oil expands once it gets hot – so when you're softening onions or vegetables you don't need to add as much as you might think. Use a vegetable oil (rapeseed or olive) non-stick cooking spray for dishes that require light frying.
- You don't need fat to add flavour – use plenty of fresh herbs and spices in your cooking. Adding a squeeze of fresh lemon juice just before serving can give food a real flavour boost.
- Bulk out savoury dishes by adding plenty of vegetables. They are low in calories and provide essential vitamins.
- Use reduced- and low-fat alternatives such as reduced-fat cheese, skimmed milk and low-fat yoghurts where available.
- To make gravies and sauces creamy, add yoghurt or fromage frais rather than cream. Stir in at the end of cooking to prevent curdling.

- Using cheese with a strong flavour, such as mature Cheddar, Parmesan or Stilton, will mean that you need to use less.
- Don't be afraid to use high-fat foods such as cheese and bacon, but you'll only need to use small quantities to add a lot of flavour.
- One tablespoon of French dressing contains 97 calories and almost 11g (¼oz) fat. Use sparingly or choose a low-fat dressing.

ESSENTIAL TIPS FOR LOSING WEIGHT FOREVER

1 / Recognise why you overeat – before you reach for a chocolate bar or slice of cake ask yourself if you're really hungry. Keep a food diary to help you identify danger times when you are more likely to overeat.

2 / Believe you can do it – a recent study found that people who believed they could lose weight and keep it off were more likely to succeed. Try to visualise the new, slimmer you and keep that image in your mind.

3 / Eat slowly and chew your food thoroughly – the brain takes 15 minutes to get the message that your stomach has had enough to eat. If you eat too quickly your stomach fills up before your brain knows you are full, and you end up eating too much.

4 / Never skip meals or allow yourself to get overhungry. If you do you'll be more tempted to snack and overeat at your next meal. Aim to eat three small to medium-sized meals a day plus 2 or 3 small, healthy snacks.

5 / Always eat breakfast – if you skip breakfast you're more likely to snack during the morning and overeat at lunch.

6 / Get fruity – fruit and vegetables are a dieter's best friend – they're low in calories and fat-free. Aim to eat at least 5 servings a day. Be adventurous and try something new. Look for recipes and ideas for new ways of cooking fruit or vegetables.

7 / Stack up with starches and fill up with fibre – choose fibre-rich varieties such as wholemeal bread and wholegrain cereals whenever possible. These provide slow-release energy which helps keep blood sugar levels stable.

8 / Be prepared – make sure your cupboards and freezer are full of healthy foods and have plenty of low-calorie snacks available.

9 / Don't feel that one bad day will ruin the whole diet – life is full of ups and downs, so if you do lapse on the odd bad day be a little stricter with yourself the following day.

10 / Never go shopping on an empty stomach – always write a list and stick to it! Don't buy foods you know you won't be able to resist.

11 / Don't deny yourself the foods you enjoy – just eat them in moderation.

12 / Drink at least 8 glasses of water a day – it's easy to confuse thirst with hunger. When you think you're feeling hungry try drinking a large glass of water first.

13 / Trim the fat – fat is a dieter's biggest enemy. Whenever possible, choose products that have less than 3% fat.

14 / Make use of every opportunity you can to stay active – use the stairs instead of the lift or escalator, get off the bus one stop early and walk the rest of the way home. Small changes all add up and can make a big difference.

HELPLINES/CONTACTS

The British Dietetic Association
5th Floor, Charles House, 148/9 Great Charles Street,
Queensway, Birmingham B3 3HT
Tel: 0121 200 8080
Website: www.bda.uk.com

Eating Disorders Association
103 Prince of Wales Road, Norwich NR1 1DW
Helpline: 01603 621 414 (open 9:00 to 18:30 weekdays)
Website: www.edauk.com

The British Nutrition Foundation
High Holborn House, 52–54 High Holborn,
London WC1V 6RQ
Tel: 020 7404 6504
Website: www.nutrition.org.uk

Weight Concern
Brook House, 2–16 Torrington Place, London WC1E 7HN
Tel: 020 7679 6636
Website: www.weightconcern.com

In many ways, breakfast is the most important meal of the day. It follows a considerable period of fasting, during which period your blood sugar levels drop, so this is a crucial time for refuelling for the hours ahead.

Breakfasts

Potentially, breakfast is a great opportunity to start a healthy eating regime, as many nutritious, low-fat foods such as cereals, fruit, porridge and yoghurts are already commonly consumed in this meal. However, beware certain varieties of these products – they can in fact be high in salt, sugar and fat, so check the nutritional information on the label.

We are not at our most culinary creative first thing in the morning, so plan ahead the night before. Aim to eat about 20–25% of your daily calorie intake at breakfast, to keep you going right through until lunchtime without the need for a mid-morning pit stop. Remember that you can add a low-fat yoghurt or a slice of dry toast to any of the dishes in this chapter for the perfect meal to start the day.

1.6% FAT | 73 CALORIES | SALT BALANCED

Watermelon, orange and ginger cocktail with granola

V | **prep** 20 minutes + 1 hour cooling/chilling | **cook** 15 minutes | **serves** 4

for the granola
10g (¼oz) rolled oats
5g (⅛oz) sesame seeds
pinch of ground ginger
5g (⅛oz) sunflower seeds
2 x 5ml sp (2tsp) freshly squeezed orange juice
1 x 5ml sp (1tsp) runny honey

for the fruit cocktail
300g (10½oz) deseeded watermelon, cut into chunks
100g (3½oz) fresh orange segments
6 x 15ml sp (6tbsp) freshly squeezed orange juice
1 x 5ml sp (1tsp) finely grated orange zest
1 x 5ml sp (1tsp) peeled and finely sliced root ginger
1 x 5ml sp (1tsp) runny honey
1 x 2.5ml sp (½tsp) arrowroot, blended with a little cold water

1. Preheat the oven to 180°C/350°F/Gas Mark 4.
2. To make the granola, put all the dry ingredients into a bowl, then add the orange juice and honey and mix thoroughly. Spread out on a non-stick baking tray and bake for 7–8 minutes. Remove from the oven, break up into pieces, then return to the oven for a further 7–8 minutes. Remove from the oven and break up again. Leave to cool on the baking sheet. The mixture will become crunchy when cool.
3. To make the fruit cocktail, put the watermelon and orange segments into a bowl. Put the orange juice and zest, ginger and honey into a small saucepan over a medium heat and bring to the boil. Gradually stir in the arrowroot mixture and cook, stirring constantly, until thickened.
4. Pour the mixture over the fruit and leave to cool, cover and chill in the fridge.
5. Spoon the covered fruit into glasses and sprinkle over the granola.

COOK'S TIPS

- *This dish can be prepared in advance and assembled just before eating.*
- *The granola will keep well in an airtight container for several days and can be used with other fruit combinations.*

NUTRITION INFORMATION
per serving

calories	fat	sat fat	salt
73	2g	0.2g	0.01g

3% FAT | 93 CALORIES | SALT BALANCED

Mini butternut squash pancakes with plum tomatoes and Parma ham

prep 10 minutes | cook 40–55 minutes | serves 4

for the pancakes
130g (4¾oz), peeled weight, butternut squash
60g (2¼oz) 0% fat natural yoghurt
1 x 5ml sp (1tsp) maple syrup
pinch of cayenne pepper
1 x 5ml sp (1tsp) rapeseed or vegetable oil
pinch of baking powder
10g (¼oz) wholemeal flour
1 medium egg white, lightly beaten
rapeseed or vegetable oil spray

for the filling
300g (10½oz) baby plum tomatoes
2 x 15ml sp (2tbsp) balsamic vinegar
1 x 5ml sp (1tsp) maple syrup
1 x 5ml sp (1tsp) finely chopped fresh thyme
4 thin slices Parma ham, all visible fat removed

1. Preheat the oven to 180°C/350°F/Gas Mark 4.
2. To make the pancakes, halve the peeled butternut squash and scoop out the seeds. Cut the flesh into chunks and spread out on a non-stick baking tray. Roast for 15–20 minutes, or until tender but not coloured.
3. Using a hand-held electric blender, blend the squash with the yoghurt, maple syrup, cayenne, oil and baking powder in a large bowl until smooth, or use a food processor. Beat in the flour, then fold in the egg white.
4. Spray a non-stick frying pan lightly with oil and heat until just smoking. Pour in a level 15ml sp (tbsp) of the batter and cook until bubbles appear on the surface. Flip over and cook for a further 1–2 minutes. Remove and keep warm. Repeat with the remaining batter. You will need 3 pancakes per serving.
5. Meanwhile, preheat the grill to hot. Halve the tomatoes, place in a large bowl with the vinegar, maple syrup and thyme and gently mix. Transfer to a non-stick baking tray and grill for 4 minutes. Add the Parma ham to the edges of the tray and grill for 2 minutes, or until crispy.
6. To serve, layer the pancakes with the tomatoes and top with the Parma ham. Drizzle over the cooking juices.

NUTRITION INFORMATION

per serving

calories	fat	sat fat	salt
93	4g	0.7g	0.2g

1% FAT | 23 CALORIES | SALT BALANCED

Mango, lime and lemon grass zinger

(V) | **prep** 10 minutes + 2 hours chilling | **serves** 4

90ml (3fl oz) freshly squeezed lime juice
25g (1oz) lemon grass, plus 2 extra stalks, peeled and halved, to garnish
1 small very ripe mango
700ml (1¼pints) low-calorie tonic water
8 ice cubes, to serve

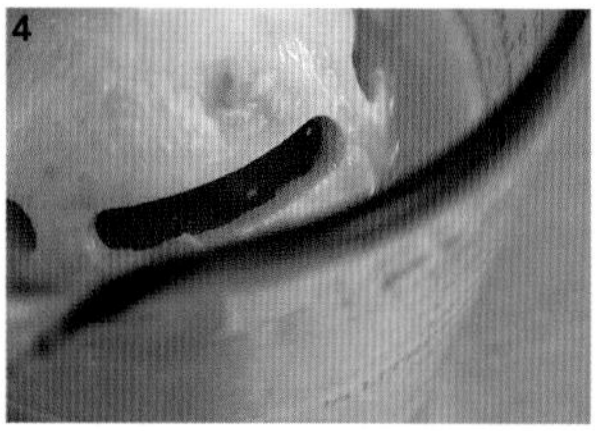

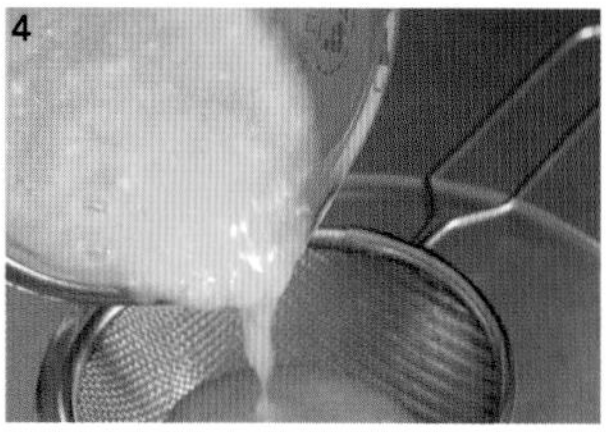

1. Pour the lime juice into a non-reactive bowl.
2. Remove the outer brown part of the lemon grass and discard. Finely shred the remaining parts and add to the lime juice.
3. Cut lengthways through the mango either side of the flat central stone. Cut away the flesh from around the stone and peel. Roughly chop the flesh and add to the bowl.
4. Using a hand-held electric blender, blend until the mango is smooth, or use a food processor. Cover the bowl with clingfilm and refrigerate for at least 2 hours before passing through a fine sieve.
5. Put a couple of ice cubes each into 4 glasses, divide the mango purée between the glasses and top up with tonic water. Add a halved lemon grass stalk to each glass to use as a stirrer.

COOK'S TIP

• *Refrigerate the mango purée overnight before passing through a sieve to extract the maximum flavour from the lemon grass.*

NUTRITION INFORMATION

per serving

calories	fat	sat fat	salt
23	0.1g	0.0g	0.002g

3% FAT | 150 CALORIES | SALT BALANCED

Spiced wholemeal muffins with marmalade and raspberry yoghurt

V | prep 15 minutes | cook 30 minutes | serves 6

rapeseed or vegetable oil spray
125g (4½oz) plain flour
1 x 2.5ml sp (½tsp) baking powder
55g (2oz) wholemeal flour
1 x 2.5ml sp (½tsp) ground mixed spice
1 x 15ml sp (1tbsp) rapeseed or vegetable oil
1 medium egg, lightly beaten
150ml (5½fl oz) buttermilk
1 x 5ml sp (1tsp) grated orange zest
1 x 15ml sp (1tbsp) freshly squeezed orange juice
1 x 5ml sp (1tsp) low-sugar marmalade, for glazing

for the filling
100g (3½oz) 0% fat Greek-style yoghurt
1 x 5ml sp (1tsp) low-sugar marmalade
1 x 2.5ml sp (½tsp) grated orange zest
100g (3½oz) fresh raspberries

1. Preheat the oven to 160°C/325°F/Gas Mark 3. Spray a six-hole muffin tin lightly with oil.
2. Sift the plain flour with the baking powder into a large mixing bowl. Using a fork, stir in the wholemeal flour and mixed spice until thoroughly mixed.
3. Pour in the oil and rub into the flour mixture with your fingertips.
4. In a separate bowl, mix the egg, buttermilk and orange zest and juice together, then pour into the centre of the flour mixture and mix with a metal spoon, being careful not to over-mix – the batter should look a little uneven and lumpy.
5. Spoon the batter into the prepared tin to come about three-quarters of the way up the sides of each hole. Bake in the oven for 30 minutes, or until golden brown and a skewer inserted into the centre of a muffin comes out clean.
6. Remove from the oven and transfer to a wire rack. Brush with the marmalade and leave to cool.
7. For the filling, mix the yoghurt with the marmalade and orange zest. Cut the warm muffins through the centre and fill with the yoghurt mixture and raspberries.

COOK'S TIP

- *These muffins are best served warm, about 30 minutes after removing from the oven, and will work well with low-sugar raspberry jam instead of marmalade if you prefer.*

NUTRITION INFORMATION

per serving

calories	fat	sat fat	salt
150	3.5g	0.5g	0.2g

Soups and salads are a fantastic way of encouraging the whole family to enjoy a wide range of fruit and vegetables. For many years, nutritionists have encouraged us to eat more fruit and vegetables, and that advice is still very current. So five a day is here to stay.

Soups, salads and

When making soups and salads, be bold with flavours and textures. Remember, for instance, that a thick, puréed type of soup will always satisfy more than a thin, clear soup and that salads with contrasting textures and interesting tastes will be far more appetising. So take a break from your routine lunchtime fare and substitute your usual sandwich for a vibrant, homemade soup, salad or pasta dish. After all, variety is the spice of life.

ight lunches

1% FAT | 93 CALORIES | SALT BALANCED

Golden pepper and yam soup

(V) **prep** 20 minutes **cook** 35 minutes **serves** 4

75g (2¾oz), peeled weight, onion, finely chopped
2 cloves garlic, peeled and finely sliced
50g (1¾oz) leek (white part only), cut into 1-cm (½-inch) cubes
50g (1¾oz) celery, cut into 1-cm (½-inch) cubes
90g (3¼oz), peeled weight, potato, cut into 1-cm (½-inch) cubes
180g (6¼oz), peeled weight, yam, cut into 1-cm (½-inch) cubes
pinch of ground turmeric
pinch of ground mace
2 bay leaves
850ml (1½pints) vegetable stock
90g (3¼oz) deseeded yellow pepper, roasted, skinned and chopped
1 x 15ml sp (1tbsp) sugar
2 x 5ml sp (2tsp) lemon juice
flat bread, to serve

for the garnish
1 x 5ml sp (1tsp) rapeseed or vegetable oil
40g (1½oz) cooked sweetcorn kernels
1 x 2.5ml sp (½tsp) habanero chilli pepper sauce

1. Put the onion, garlic, leek and celery into a large, lidded saucepan over a high heat and cook, stirring constantly, for 5 minutes, or until softened but not coloured. You will not need any oil as the steam and the continuous stirring will prevent the vegetables from sticking.
2. Add the potato, yam, turmeric, mace, bay leaves and stock, stir well and bring to the boil. Reduce the heat, cover and simmer for 20 minutes, or until all the vegetables are soft.
3. Meanwhile, in a separate pan, heat the oil, add the sweetcorn and stir-fry until golden brown. Remove from the heat and stir in the chilli sauce. Reserve for garnishing the soup.
4. Remove the bay leaves from the soup and discard. Stir in the roasted pepper, sugar and lemon juice. Using a hand-held electric blender, blend the soup until smooth, or use a food processor.
5. Ladle into warmed soup bowls, sprinkle with the sweetcorn garnish and serve, accompanied by flat bread.

NUTRITION INFORMATION
per serving

calories	fat	sat fat	salt
93	1g	0.1g	0.5g

2% FAT | 97 CALORIES | SALT BALANCED

Creamy butter bean, porcini and tarragon soup

V | **prep** 15 minutes + 8 hours soaking | **cook** 1 hour 55 minutes | **serves** 4

70g (2½oz) leek (white part only), cut into 1-cm (½-inch) cubes
100g (3½oz), peeled weight, onion, cut into 1-cm (½-inch) cubes
70g (2½oz) celery, cut into 1-cm (½-inch) cubes
1 clove garlic, peeled and crushed
2 bay leaves
150g (5½oz) fresh flat mushrooms, cut into 1-cm (½-inch) cubes, plus 2tbsp diced to garnish
15g (½oz) dried porcini mushrooms, soaked in 50ml (2fl oz) hot water and drained
85g (3oz), peeled weight, potato, cut into 1-cm (½-inch) cubes
115g (4oz) canned butter beans, drained and rinsed under cold water
700ml (1¼pints) vegetable stock
1 x 15ml sp (1tbsp) chopped fresh tarragon, plus extra to garnish
125ml (4fl oz) skimmed milk

for the garnish
2 x 5ml sp (2tsp) lemon juice
1½ x 5ml sp (1½tsp) sugar
pinch of freshly ground black pepper
3 x 15ml sp (3tbsp) 0% fat fromage frais

1. Put the leek, onion, celery and garlic into a large saucepan over a high heat and cook, stirring constantly, for 5 minutes, or until softened but not coloured. You will not need any oil as the steam and the continuous stirring will prevent the vegetables from sticking.
2. Add the bay leaves, mushrooms, potato, beans, stock and tarragon, stir well and bring to the boil. Reduce the heat, cover and simmer for 20 minutes, or until the vegetables are mushy.
3. Meanwhile, for the garnish, mix the lemon juice, sugar and pepper together in a separate saucepan. Add the diced mushroom, cover and cook over a high heat for 4–5 minutes. Remove from the heat and leave to cool in the pan.
4. Remove the bay leaves from the soup and discard. Using a hand-held electric blender, blend the soup until smooth, or use a food processor. Stir in the milk. Pass through a medium sieve into a serving dish.
5. To serve, pour the mushroom garnish into the soup, sprinkle over a little tarragon and add a swirl of fromage frais.

NUTRITION INFORMATION

per serving

calories	fat	sat fat	salt
97	0.8g	0.1g	0.5g

0.5% FAT | 60 CALORIES | SALT BALANCED

Chickpea, saffron and lemon chermoula soup

V | **prep** 25 minutes + 8 hours soaking | **cook** 2 hours 10 minutes | **serves** 6

50g (1¾oz) leek, cut into 1-cm (½-inch) cubes
100g (3½oz), peeled weight, onion, cut into 1-cm (½-inch) cubes
50g (1¾oz) celery, cut into 1-cm (½-inch) cubes
85g (3oz), peeled weight, carrot, cut into 1-cm (½-inch) cubes
2 cloves garlic, peeled and crushed
1 x 15ml sp (1tbsp) coriander seeds
115g (4oz) tomatoes
140g (5oz) canned chickpeas, drained and rinsed under cold water
1litre (1¾pints) vegetable stock
100g (3½oz), peeled weight, potato, cut into 1-cm (½-inch) cubes
2 bay leaves
pinch of strands saffron
2 lemons, halved, cut sides charred for 2–5 minutes in a hot non-stick frying pan

for the chermoula

2 cloves garlic, peeled and finely sliced
½ red chilli, finely chopped
1 x 5ml sp (1tsp) paprika
1 x 5ml sp (1tsp) ground cumin
1 x 5ml sp (1tsp) lemon juice
2 x 5ml sp (2tsp) white wine vinegar
4 x 15ml sp (4tbsp) finely chopped fresh flat-leaved parsley
4 x 15ml sp (4tbsp) finely chopped fresh coriander leaves

1. Put the leek, onion, celery, carrot and garlic into a large, lidded saucepan over a high heat and cook, stirring constantly, for 5 minutes, or until softened but not coloured. (You will not need any oil.) Add the coriander seeds and cook for a further 2 minutes.
2. Add the tomatoes, chickpeas, stock, potato, bay leaves and saffron, stir well and bring to the boil. Reduce the heat, cover and simmer for 20 minutes, or until the vegetables are mushy.
3. To make the chermoula, pound the garlic with the spices, lemon juice and vinegar to a smooth paste in a mortar with a pestle. Transfer to a saucepan, add the herbs and gently warm for 5 minutes to infuse the flavours. Do not boil.
4. Remove the bay leaves, then blend the soup using a hand-held blender, or use a food processor. Pass through a medium sieve into warmed serving bowls. Top with the chermoula and serve with the charred lemons for squeezing over.

COOK'S TIP

- *Using the charred lemons for the seasoning gives a similar flavour to pickled lemons, which taste great but have a very high salt content.*

NUTRITION INFORMATION

per serving

calories	fat	sat fat	salt
60	1g	0.1g	0.5g

2% FAT | 142 CALORIES | SALT BALANCED

Gazpacho with crab, spring onion and crème fraîche

prep 15 minutes | **serves** 2

for the gazpacho

70g (2½oz) deseeded red pepper, cut into 1-cm (½-inch) squares
50g (1¾oz) deseeded green pepper, cut into 1-cm (½-inch) squares
70g (2½oz), peeled weight, onion, cut into 1-cm (½-inch) cubes
200g (7oz) tomatoes
100g (3½oz) cucumber
1 x 15ml sp (1tbsp) red wine vinegar
2 x 15ml sp (2tbsp) freshly squeezed orange juice
2 x 15ml sp (2tbsp) freshly squeezed lemon juice
1 clove garlic, peeled and finely sliced
pinch of paprika
pinch of cayenne pepper
pinch of freshly ground black pepper

for the garnish

40g (1½oz) 0% fat fromage frais
25g (1oz) 15% fat crème fraîche
10g (¼oz) spring onion, finely sliced
25g (1oz) cooked white crabmeat
2 x 5ml sp (2tsp) extra virgin olive oil

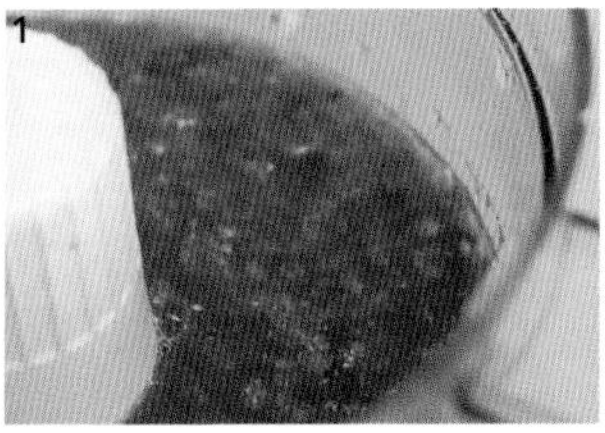

1. Put all the ingredients for the gazpacho into a large bowl. Using a hand-held electric blender, blend until smooth, or use a food processor.
2. To prepare the garnish, mix the fromage frais, crème fraîche, spring onion and crabmeat together in a small bowl. Cover and store in the fridge until ready to serve.
3. To serve, pour the soup into serving bowls, then top with the crabmeat mixture and drizzle over the oil.

NUTRITION INFORMATION

per serving

calories	fat	sat fat	salt
142	6g	2g	0.16g

1.3% FAT | 107 CALORIES | SALT BALANCED

Potato, herb and smoked salmon gratin

prep 25 minutes + 20 minutes cooling | **cook** 50 minutes | **serves** 6

400ml (14fl oz) semi-skimmed milk
3 whole cloves
2 bay leaves
50g (1¾oz), peeled weight, onion, sliced
85g (3oz) leek, chopped
100g (3½oz) lightly cured smoked salmon, finely sliced into strips
350g (12oz), peeled weight, potatoes, cut into 2-mm (1/16-inch) slices
2 x 15ml sp (2tbsp) finely chopped fresh chives
2 x 15ml sp (2tbsp) finely chopped fresh dill
1 x 15ml sp (1tbsp) finely chopped fresh tarragon
2 x 5ml sp (2tsp) wholegrain mustard
freshly ground black pepper, to taste
35g (1¼oz) watercress

1. Preheat the oven to 200°C/400°F/Gas Mark 6. Line the base of a 19-cm (7½-inch) sandwich tin with greaseproof paper.
2. Pour the milk into a large, heavy-based saucepan, add the cloves, bay leaves, onion, leek and smoked salmon and heat over a low heat.
3. When the milk is just about to reach simmering point, carefully remove the smoked salmon with a slotted spoon and leave to cool on a plate.
4. Add the potatoes to the milk and stir with a wooden spoon. Return to a simmer and cook, stirring occasionally to prevent the potatoes from sticking, for 12 minutes, or until the potatoes are just beginning to soften and the milk has thickened slightly from the potato starch. Remove the cloves and bay leaves.
5. Add the herbs, mustard and pepper and stir well. Pour the mixture into the prepared tin. Cover with a layer of greaseproof paper and then foil and bake in the oven for 30 minutes.
6. Remove from the oven and place a saucepan on top. Leave to cool for 20 minutes before turning out onto a baking sheet. Put under a preheated hot grill to brown the top. Cut the gratin into 6 wedges and serve with the smoked salmon, tossed with the watercress.

COOK'S TIP

- *This gratin can be made in advance and then quickly reheated in the microwave to serve.*

NUTRITION INFORMATION

per serving

calories	fat	sat fat	salt
107	2g	0.8g	0.9g

2% FAT | 245 CALORIES | SALT BALANCED

Tagliatelle with roasted artichokes and horseradish-herb sauce

V | prep 15 minutes | cook 35 minutes | serves 2

100g (3½oz), drained weight, canned artichokes, quartered
vegetable oil spray
50g (1¾oz) fresh baby spinach leaves
100g (3½oz) dried tagliatelle
100ml (3½fl oz) White Sauce (see below)
2 x 5ml sp (2tsp) chopped fresh basil, plus extra to garnish
1 x 5ml sp (1tsp) finely chopped fresh lemon thyme, plus extra to garnish
1 x 5ml sp (1tsp) creamed horseradish
2 x 5ml sp (2tsp) 15% fat crème fraîche

1. Preheat the oven to 220°C/425°F/Gas Mark 7.
2. Spread the artichokes out on a non-stick baking tray, spray lightly with oil and roast in the oven for 20 minutes until golden brown.
3. Meanwhile, heat a large, lidded saucepan over a medium heat. Add the spinach, cover and steam for 2 minutes. Remove from the heat and drain the spinach in a colander.
4. Cook the pasta according to the instructions on the packet and drain.
5. Return the drained spinach to the pan, add the sauce and warm gently. Add the herbs, horseradish, crème fraîche and artichokes and stir in the warm pasta. Allow to warm through.
6. Serve, garnished with extra herbs.

NUTRITION INFORMATION

per serving

calories	fat	sat fat	salt
245	4.5g	0.6g	0.3g

White sauce

V | prep 5 minutes | cook 10 minutes | serves 2

250ml (9fl oz) skimmed milk
20g (¾oz) cornflour
1 x 5ml sp (1tsp) mustard powder
2 small bay leaves
1 small onion
4 x 5ml sp (4tsp) freshly grated vegetarian Parmesan or Pecorino cheese
120g (4¼oz) baby spinach leaves

1. To make the sauce, put the milk into a small non-stick saucepan with the flour, mustard, onion and bay leaf. Whisk over a medium heat until thick. Remove from the heat, discard the onion and bay leaf and stir in the cheese. Set aside, stirring occasionally, to prevent a skin forming.

1.5% FAT | 291 CALORIES | SALT BALANCED

Pasta with spiced leek, butternut squash and cherry tomatoes

V | prep 15 minutes | cook 25 minutes | serves 4

150g (5½oz) baby leeks, cut into 2-cm (¾-inch) slices
175g (6oz), peeled weight, butternut squash, deseeded and cut into 2-cm (¾-inch) chunks
1½ x 15ml sp (1½tbsp) medium ready-prepared curry paste
1 x 5ml sp (1tsp) rapeseed or vegetable oil
175g (6oz) cherry tomatoes
250g (9oz) dried pasta of your choice
300ml (½pint) White Sauce (see page 45)
2 x 15ml sp (2tbsp) chopped fresh coriander leaves

1. Preheat the oven to 200°C/400°F/Gas Mark 6.
2. Bring a large saucepan of water to the boil, add the leeks and cook for 2 minutes. Add the butternut squash and cook for a further 2 minutes. Drain in a colander.
3. Mix the curry paste with the oil in a large bowl. Toss the leeks and butternut squash in the mixture to coat thoroughly.
4. Transfer the leeks and butternut squash to a non-stick baking tray and roast in the oven for 10 minutes until golden brown. Add the tomatoes and roast for a further 5 minutes.
5. Meanwhile, cook the pasta according to the instructions on the packet and drain.
6. Put the sauce into a large saucepan and warm over a low heat. Add the leeks, butternut squash, tomatoes and coriander and stir in the warm pasta. Mix thoroughly and serve.

NUTRITION INFORMATION

per serving

calories	fat	sat fat	salt
291	3g	0.5g	0.25g

1% FAT | 134 CALORIES | SALT BALANCED

Thai chicken salad

prep 30 minutes + 2 hours standing | **cook** 15 minutes | **serves** 6

vegetable oil spray
115g (4oz) skinless chicken breast, cut lengthways horizontally
3 limes, halved, for squeezing over

for the dressing
1 x 15ml sp (1tbsp) finely shredded lemon grass
1 small green chilli, finely chopped
3 x 15ml sp (3tbsp) lime juice
1-cm (½-inch) galangal or root ginger, peeled and thinly sliced into strips
1½ x 5ml sp (1½tsp) sugar
2 x 15ml sp (2tbsp) white wine vinegar
90ml (3fl oz) water
1½ x 5ml sp (1½tsp) cornflour, blended with a little cold water

for the salad
50g (1¾oz) deseeded mixed peppers, finely sliced into strips
50g (1¾oz), peeled weight, carrot, finely sliced into strips
50g (1¾oz) courgette, finely sliced into strips
50g (1¾oz) mangetout, finely sliced into strips
50g (1¾oz) baby corn cobs, finely sliced into strips
50g (1¾oz) broccoli florets, cut into 5-mm (¼-inch) pieces
50g (1¾oz) pak choi, shredded
4 x 15ml sp (4tbsp) roughly chopped fresh coriander leaves
25g (1oz) rice vermicelli, covered with boiling water, left to cool in the water and drained

1. To make the dressing, put all the dressing ingredients, except the cornflour, into a small saucepan over a low heat and bring to the boil. Gradually add the cornflour mixture, stirring constantly, and cook until thickened. Remove from the heat and leave to cool.
2. Heat a griddle pan over a high heat and spray lightly with oil. Add the chicken and cook for 2 minutes on each side, or until thoroughly cooked through. Remove the chicken from the pan and shred.
3. To make the salad, put all the salad ingredients with the chicken into a large bowl. Pour over the dressing and toss together, making sure that all the ingredients are well coated.
4. Cover and refrigerate for at least 2 hours before serving. Serve on large plates, squeezing the juice from half a lime over each portion.

NUTRITION INFORMATION

per serving

calories	fat	sat fat	salt
134	1.5g	0.4g	0.3g

2% FAT | 111 CALORIES | SALT BALANCED

Stuffed aubergines with ruby chard and spinach salad

(V) | prep 40 minutes + 8 hours soaking | cook 2 hours | serves 4

175g (6oz) canned borlotti beans
250g (9oz) cherry tomatoes, halved
8 baby aubergines, or 2 aubergines, halved
vegetable oil spray
1 x 2.5ml sp (½tsp) cumin seeds
1 x 2.5ml sp (½tsp) coriander seeds
2 x 5ml sp (2tsp) ground cinnamon
1 x 1.25ml sp (¼tsp) dried marjoram
2 x 5ml (2tsp) crushed garlic
1 x 2.5ml sp (½tsp) finely chopped red chilli
1 x 2.5ml sp (½tsp) vegetable oil
50g (2oz), peeled weight, onion, finely chopped
3 x 15ml sp (3tbsp) chopped fresh dill
3 x 15ml sp (3tbsp) chopped fresh mint
juice 1 lemon
freshly ground black pepper, to taste

for the salad

1 x 15ml sp (1tbsp) white wine vinegar
freshly ground black pepper, to taste
pinch of cayenne pepper
1 x 15ml sp (1tbsp) extra virgin olive oil
60g (2¼oz) mixed ruby chard and fresh spinach leaves

1. Drain the beans and rinse under cold water for 2 minutes to remove the salt.
2. Preheat the oven to 190°C/375°F/Gas Mark 5.
3. Arrange the tomatoes and aubergines in a roasting tin, spray lightly with vegetable oil and roast in the oven for 7–8 minutes. Remove the tomatoes and cool on a plate. Roast the aubergines for a further 10–12 minutes, or until tender.
4. Meanwhile, pound the cumin and coriander seeds, cinnamon, marjoram, garlic and chilli to a smooth paste in a mortar with a pestle.
5. Remove the aubergines from the oven, leave to cool slightly, then cut in half lengthways and scoop the flesh into a bowl using a teaspoon, reserving the skins.
6. Heat a non-stick frying pan over a medium heat, add the vegetable oil and fry the onion until golden brown. Add the spice paste and cook for 2 minutes. Add the aubergine pulp, beans, herbs, lemon juice and pepper and mash together using a fork. Remove from the heat and leave to cool.
7. Put 100g (3½oz) of the cherry tomatoes into a bowl with the vinegar, pepper, cayenne and olive oil and blend with a hand-held electric blender, or use a food processor. Pass the dressing through a fine sieve.
8. Fill the aubergine skins with the bean mixture, then place 2 tomato halves on each filled skin and transfer to a non-stick baking tray. Heat in the oven for 10 minutes.
9. Arrange the ruby chard and spinach on a serving plate, drizzle with the tomato dressing and top with the aubergines.

NUTRITION INFORMATION

per serving

calories	fat	sat fat	salt
111	5g	0.7g	0.6g

2.5% FAT | 15 CALORIES | SALT BALANCED

Roasted pepper and garlic dressing

V | prep 15 minutes | cook 30 minutes | serves 8

85g (3oz) deseeded red pepper, halved
1 x 2.5ml sp (½tsp) rapeseed or vegetable oil
2 x 15ml sp (2tbsp) sliced garlic
1 x 15ml sp (1tbsp) coriander seeds
1 x 5ml sp (1tsp) cumin seeds
2 x 5ml (2tsp) chopped fresh rosemary
100ml (3½fl oz) water
1 x 5ml sp (1tsp) sugar
1 x 1.25ml sp (¼tsp) smoked paprika
1 x 15ml sp (1tbsp) white wine vinegar
1 x 15ml sp (1tbsp) cornflour, blended with a little cold water

1. Preheat the oven to 200°C/400°F/Gas Mark 6. Put the pepper on a non-stick baking tray and roast in the oven until the skin blisters. Remove from the oven, leave to cool, then peel off the skin.
2. Heat the oil in a small saucepan over a medium heat, add the garlic and cook, stirring constantly, until golden brown. Add the coriander and cumin and cook for 1 minute, stirring. Add the rosemary, water, sugar, paprika and vinegar and bring to the boil. Gradually add the cornflour, stirring constantly, and cook until thickened.
3. Add the roasted pepper. Using a hand-held electric blender, blend until smooth, or use a food processor.
4. Pass through a fine sieve, cover with clingfilm to prevent a skin forming and leave to cool.
5. Keep the dressing in the fridge. Serve tossed with mixed leaves to accompany grilled chicken and fish dishes.

NUTRITION INFORMATION

per serving

calories	fat	sat fat	salt
15	0.6g	0.0g	0.005g

1% FAT | 13 CALORIES | SALT BALANCED

Pink grapefruit, raspberry, wasabi and pumpkin seed oil dressing

V | prep 15 minutes | cook 5 minutes | serves 12

1 pink grapefruit
75ml (2½fl oz) water
1 x 15ml sp (1tbsp) white wine vinegar
1 x 5ml sp (1tsp) sugar
1 x 15ml sp (1tbsp) cornflour, blended with a little cold water
25g (1oz) raspberries
1 x 1.25ml sp (¼tsp) wasabi paste
1 x 5ml sp (1tsp) toasted sesame seed oil

1. Working over a bowl to catch the juice, halve the grapefruit, then cut out the segments between the membranes. Weigh out and reserve 85g (3oz) segments. Squeeze and measure out 85ml (3fl oz) juice from the remaining grapefruit segments.
2. Put the grapefruit juice, water, vinegar and sugar into a small saucepan over a medium heat and bring to the boil.
3. Gradually add the cornflour mixture, stirring constantly, and cook until thickened. Remove from the heat and add the reserved grapefruit segments, raspberries, wasabi paste and oil.
4. Using a hand-held electric blender, blend the mixture until smooth, or use a food processor. Pass through a fine sieve. Cover with clingfilm to prevent a skin forming and chill in the fridge. Keep the dressing in the fridge until ready to use.
5. Use with shredded vegetables or fruits to make a delicious salad, or as a sauce to accompany salmon dishes.

NUTRITION INFORMATION

per serving

calories	fat	sat fat	salt
13	0.3g	0.0g	0.005g

2% FAT | 165 CALORIES | SALT BALANCED

Spiced lamb and butternut burger with saffron and cucumber raita

prep 30 minutes + 1 hour cooling/chilling | cook 30–35 minutes | serves 2

for the burgers

50g (1¾oz), peeled weight, butternut squash, deseeded and cut into 5-mm (¼-inch) cubes
2 small cloves crushed garlic
40g (1½oz) peeled weight, onion, finely chopped
1 x 15ml sp (1tbsp) chopped fresh basil
pinch of ground cumin
pinch of crushed coriander seeds
pinch of chilli powder
1 x 2.5ml sp (½tsp) dried marjoram
½ egg white
75g (2¾oz) leg of lamb, all visible fat removed, minced or finely chopped

for the raita

50g (1¾oz) cucumber
4 x 15ml sp (4tbsp) 0% fat Greek-style yoghurt
pinch of strands saffron, soaked in a little warm water for 15 minutes

for the garnish

1 beef tomato, halved
1 small wholemeal bread roll, halved
15g (½oz) mixed salad leaves
½ lemon, for squeezing over the burgers

1. Preheat the oven to 180°C/350°F/Gas Mark 4.
2. Spread the butternut squash out on a non-stick baking tray and cook in the oven for 15–20 minutes, or until tender. Remove and cool on a plate.
3. Meanwhile, to make the raita, grate the cucumber into a small bowl, add the yoghurt and saffron and mix together. Cover and chill in the fridge.
4. Dry-sweat the garlic and onion in a frying pan for 3-4 minutes, or until soft.
5. Using a fork, mash the cold butternut squash in a bowl, then add the basil, cumin, coriander, chilli powder, marjoram, egg white and lamb together with the garlic and onion. Mix thoroughly, form into 2 equal-sized burgers and put on a non-stick baking tray.
6. Preheat the grill. Grill the burgers and tomato for 4–5 minutes on each side, or until the burgers are cooked through and the tomato is golden brown.
7. Lightly toast the bread roll halves.
8. Serve each burger on a bread roll half with the grilled tomato and salad leaves. Squeeze over a little lemon. Serve the raita separately.

NUTRITION INFORMATION

per serving

calories	fat	sat fat	salt
165	4.5g	2g	0.6g

In Britain, most of us still consider that meat and fish should constitute the main part of a meal, but in fact we all tend to eat far too much protein and the body needs a lot less than we imagine. Consider the food on your plate as a whole

Meat and fish main

picture, with meat or fish forming just one part of a healthy, nutritious meal. If you divide your plate into three equal segments of protein, carbohydrates and vegetables, you will achieve a more balanced approach to eating. It is also important that the flavours of all three components complement each other and that they are achieved as naturally as possible.

Always choose the freshest, best-quality meat and fish you can buy to enjoy their natural flavours to the full. We have become over-reliant on one seasoning in particular, salt, which is not only over-used in processed food but during cooking and at the table. Use healthy alternatives such as citrus juices, vinegars spices and herbs. You will be surprised how quickly your body stops craving salt and within a couple of weeks you will find yourself no longer needing to reach for the salt pot.

courses

2% FAT | 348 CALORIES | SALT BALANCED

Chicken kebabs with Asian coleslaw, fragrant rice and spicy dipping sauce

prep 30 minutes + 1 hour marinating/soaking/cooling | **cook** 10 minutes | **serves** 2

175g (6oz) chicken fillets
100g (3½oz), dry weight, fragrant Thai rice
vegetable oil spray

for the chicken marinade
1 x 15ml sp (1tbsp) finely chopped lemon grass
1 x 5ml sp (1tsp) grated root ginger
1 x 2.5ml sp (½tsp) grated garlic
1 x 1.25ml sp (¼tsp) ground turmeric
1 x 2.5ml sp (½tsp) finely chopped red chilli
1 x 15ml sp (1tbsp) lime juice
1 x 2.5ml sp (½tsp) sugar

for the dipping sauce
100ml (3½fl oz) unsweetened pineapple juice
1 x 15ml sp (1tbsp) white wine vinegar
1 x 1.25ml sp (¼tsp) grated root ginger
1 x 2.5ml sp (½tsp) finely chopped red chilli
1 x 15ml sp (1tbsp) finely chopped spring onion
1 x 2.5ml sp (½tsp) arrowroot, blended with a little cold water
1 x 1.25ml sp (¼tsp) toasted sesame oil
1 x 15ml sp (1tbsp) chopped fresh coriander leaves

for the coleslaw
50g (1¾oz) pak choi, shredded
40g (1½oz), peeled weight, carrot, finely sliced into strips
60g (2¼oz), peeled weight, mooli, finely sliced into strips
40g (1½oz) deseeded red pepper, finely sliced into strips

1. To make the marinade, mix all the ingredients together in a large bowl. Add the chicken fillets and toss well to coat. Cover and leave to marinate in the fridge for 30 minutes, turning occasionally.
2. Meanwhile, to make the dipping sauce, put all the ingredients, except the arrowroot mixture, sesame oil and coriander, into a small saucepan over a medium heat and bring to the boil. Using a hand whisk, gradually beat the arrowroot mixture into the boiling liquid, whisking constantly until thickened. Remove the pan from the heat and stir in the sesame oil and coriander. Leave to cool.
3. Soak 6 bamboo skewers in cold water for 30 minutes, then thread the chicken fillets, concertina-style, onto the skewers. Cover and refrigerate until ready to cook.
4. Cook the rice according to the instructions on the packet and drain.
5. Meanwhile, to make the coleslaw, mix all the ingredients together in a large bowl with half the dipping sauce, then spoon onto a serving dish.
6. Preheat the grill to hot. Transfer the chicken skewers to a non-stick baking sheet and grill for 4 minutes on each side, or until cooked through. Serve on top of the coleslaw, with the rice and dipping sauce served separately.

NUTRITION INFORMATION
per serving

calories	fat	sat fat	salt
348	6g	1.5g	0.3g

2% FAT | 250 CALORIES | SALT BALANCED

Duck breast with noodles and crunchy rice topping

prep 35 minutes + 10 minutes soaking | cook 1¼ hours | serves 4

160ml (2¾fl oz) freshly squeezed orange juice
200ml (3½fl oz) water
1 x 10ml sp (2tsp) crushed garlic
1 x 5ml sp (1tsp) finely chopped root ginger
2 star anise
1 x 1.25ml sp (¼tsp) sechuan pepper
2 x 5ml sp (2tsp) grated orange zest
1 x 5ml sp (1tsp) sugar
2 duck breasts, skin and any visible fat removed
20g (¾oz), dry weight, white rice
1 x 2.5ml sp (½tsp) cornflour, blended with a little cold water
1 x 2.5ml sp (½tsp) sesame oil
100g (3½oz) Chinese leaf, shredded
150g (5½oz) beansprouts
150g (5½oz) mixed deseeded peppers, finely sliced into strips
25g (1oz) spring onion, finely sliced into strips
240g (8¾oz), dry weight, egg noodles, refreshed in cold water and drained

for the garnish
4 x 15ml sp (4tbsp) shredded spring onion
4 x 15ml sp (4tbsp) chopped fresh coriander leaves

1. Preheat the oven to 200°C/400°F/Gas Mark 6.
2. Put the orange juice, water, garlic, ginger, spices, orange zest and sugar into a small saucepan and bring to the boil. Reduce the heat and simmer for 3–4 minutes.
3. Lay the duck in a small, ovenproof dish and pour over the orange mixture. Cover with a tight-fitting lid or foil and cook in the oven for 1 hour.
4. Soak the rice in cold water for 10 minutes, drain and pat dry with kitchen paper. Heat a small, non-stick frying pan over a medium heat, add the rice and dry-fry until golden brown. Remove from the heat, tip on to one half of a clean tea towel, then fold the other half over the rice. Using a rolling pin, crush into fine grains.
5. Remove the duck from the cooking liquid with a slotted spoon, shred and keep warm. Transfer the cooking liquid to a saucepan over a medium heat. Gradually add the cornflour mixture, stirring constantly, and cook until thickened. Pass through a sieve into a bowl and keep warm.
6. Heat a wok over a high heat, then add the oil. Add the vegetables and stir-fry for a few minutes until cooked. Add the noodles, duck and sauce and briefly stir-fry. Serve in warmed bowls, garnished with spring onion and coriander and sprinkled with the rice.

NUTRITION INFORMATION

per serving

calories	fat	sat fat	salt
250	6.5g	2g	0.3g

2% FAT | 200 CALORIES | SALT BALANCED

Braised lamb with pea salsa and quinoa tabbouleh

prep 30 minutes | cook 1 hour | serves 4

4 x 60g (2¼oz) leg of lamb steaks, all visible fat removed
50g (1¾oz), peeled weight, onion, finely chopped
1 clove garlic, peeled and finely chopped
2 bay leaves
2 sprigs of rosemary
100ml (3½fl oz) water
2 x 15ml sp (2tbsp) red wine
250ml (9fl oz) passata

for the pea salsa
40g (1½oz) French beans, cut into 5-mm (¼-inch) pieces
40g (1½oz) shelled peas
40g (1½oz) sugar snap peas, cut into 5-mm (¼-inch) pieces
40g (1½oz) mangetout, cut into 5-mm (¼-inch) pieces
2 x 15ml sp (2tbsp) balsamic vinegar
1 x 2.5ml sp (½tsp) Dijon mustard

for the quinoa tabbouleh
600ml (1pint) water
50g (1¾oz), dry weight, quinoa
50g (1¾oz), dry weight, bulgar wheat
1 x 5ml sp (1tsp) ready-made mint sauce from a jar
1 x 15ml sp (1tbsp) lemon juice
50g (1¾oz) tomato, skinned, deseeded and cut into 5-mm (¼-inch) pieces

1. Preheat the oven to 180°C/350°F/Gas Mark 4.
2. Using a rolling pin or mallet, gently beat the lamb steaks between 2 layers of clingfilm to 2mm (1/16inch) thick, then roll up to form olives, folding in the ends to neaten.
3. Heat a flame-proof casserole dish over a medium heat, add the onion, garlic, bay leaves and rosemary and cook until the onion is softened. Add the 100ml (3½fl oz) water, wine and passata, then lay the olives on top and bring to the boil. Cover and cook in the oven for 45 minutes, or until the meat is tender.
4. Meanwhile, to make the salsa, blanch the vegetables, refresh in cold water until cold and drain. Mix the vinegar and mustard together in a microwave-proof container, add the vegetables and toss to coat.
5. Bring the 600ml (1pint) water to the boil in a saucepan, add the quinoa and bulgar wheat and cook for 12 minutes. Drain, tip into a separate microwave-proof container with the mint sauce, lemon juice and tomato and mix well.
6. Remove the olives from the casserole with a slotted spoon and keep warm. Reduce the sauce over a high heat until thick and syrupy.
7. Reheat the tabbouleh and salsa in a microwave oven on full power for 1½ minutes. Put the olives on top of the tabbouleh, pour over the sauce and serve with salsa.

NUTRITION INFORMATION

per serving

calories	fat	sat fat	salt
200	4g	1.5g	0.4g

2.5% FAT | 300 CALORIES | SALT BALANCED

Lean 'n' mean Jamaican jerk pork cutlets with rice, black-eyed beans and roasted squash

prep 20 minutes | **cook** 30 minutes | **serves** 4

85g (3oz), peeled weight, onion, finely chopped
85g (3oz) deseeded red pepper, cut into 5-mm (¼-inch) squares
2 bay leaves
2 blades mace
60g (2¼oz) easy-cook long-grain rice
350ml (12fl oz) chicken stock
85g (3oz) cooked black-eyed beans
freshly ground black pepper, to taste
275g (9½oz) squash, deseeded but left unpeeled and cut into 1-cm (½-inch) wedges
4 x 115g (4oz) pork loin chops, all visible fat removed and the bone trimmed
rapeseed or vegetable oil spray
½ lemon, cut into wedges, for squeezing over

for the jerk spice rub

1 x 5ml sp (1tsp) sugar
1 x 2.5ml sp (½tsp) dried oregano
1 x 2.5ml sp (½tsp) paprika
1 x 2.5ml sp (½tsp) ground cinnamon
1 x 1.25ml sp (¼tsp) chilli powder
1 x 2.5ml sp (½tsp) crushed garlic
1 x 1.25ml sp (¼tsp) ground allspice
1 x 15ml sp (1tbsp) lemon juice

1. Preheat the oven to 200°C/400°F/Gas Mark 6.
2. Heat a medium, lidded saucepan over a high heat, add the onion and pepper and cook for 2 minutes, stirring constantly. Add the bay leaves and mace, then stir in the rice, stock, beans and pepper. Cover, bring to a simmer and cook for 12–15 minutes, or until the rice has absorbed the stock and is tender. Remove from the heat and keep warm.
3. Meanwhile, spread the squash out on a non-stick baking tray and cook in the oven for 15 minutes, turning occasionally, until golden brown.
4. To make the jerk spice rub, mix all the ingredients in a bowl and rub into the pork.
5. Heat a griddle pan over a medium heat and spray lightly with oil. Sear the chops on both sides, then cook for 4–5 minutes on each side, or until thoroughly cooked through. Do not allow the pan to become too hot as it will burn the spice mix before the meat is cooked.
6. Serve the cutlets with the rice and beans and the roasted squash, squeezing the lemon over the meat.

NUTRITION INFORMATION

per serving

calories	fat	sat fat	salt
300	9g	3g	0.7g

1% FAT | 150 CALORIES | SALT BALANCED

Sweet and sour sea bass

prep 25 minutes + 30 minutes cooling | cook 15 minutes | serves 2

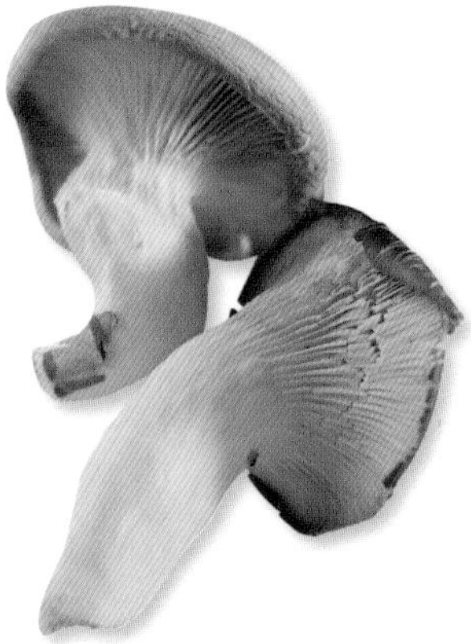

60g (2¼oz) pak choi, shredded
40g (1½oz) beansprouts
40g (1½oz) shiitake mushrooms, sliced
40g (1½oz) oyster mushrooms, torn
20g (¾oz) spring onion, finely sliced
1 x 5ml sp (1tsp) finely grated root ginger
1 x 15ml sp (1tbsp) finely sliced lemon grass
2 x 90g (2 x 3¼oz) sea bass fillets, skinned and boned
10g (¼oz) sesame seeds, toasted

for the sweet and sour sauce
90ml (3fl oz) unsweetened pineapple juice
1 x 15ml sp (1tbsp) sugar
1 x 15ml sp (1tbsp) red wine vinegar
2 star anise, crushed
90ml (3fl oz) tomato juice
1 x 15ml sp (1tbsp) cornflour, blended with a little cold water

1. Preheat the oven to 200°C/400°F/Gas Mark 6. Cut 2 x 38cm (15inch) squares of greaseproof paper and 2 of the same size aluminium foil squares.
2. To make the sauce, heat the pineapple juice, sugar, red wine vinegar, star anise and tomato juice, simmer for 1–2 minutes then thicken with the cornflour and water mixture, whisking continuously, then pass through a fine sieve into a small bowl to cool.
3. In a separate large bowl mix together the pak choi, beansprouts, mushrooms and spring onions, then add the ginger and lemon grass. Toss all the ingredients together.
4. Put a square of greaseproof paper on top of a square of foil and fold into a triangle. Open up and place half the vegetable mix into the centre, pour half the sweet and sour sauce over the vegetables and place the sea bass on top. Sprinkle with a few sesame seeds. Close the triangle over the mixture and, starting at the top, fold the right corner and crumple the edges together to form an airtight triangular bag. Repeat to make the second bag.
5. Place onto a baking tray and cook in the oven for 10 minutes until the foil bags puff with steam. To serve, place on individual plates and snip open at the table so that you can enjoy the wonderful aromas as the bag is opened.

NUTRITION INFORMATION

per serving

calories	fat	sat fat	salt
150	3g	0.5g	0.05g

1.5% FAT | 100 CALORIES | SALT BALANCED

Blackened snapper with sweetcorn papaya relish

prep 20 minutes + 45 minutes cooling | **cook** 20 minutes | **serves** 4

4 x 85g (3oz) snapper fillets
vegetable oil spray
2 lemons, halved, to serve

for the relish
2 x 15ml sp (2tbsp) finely chopped onion
1 x 5ml sp (1tsp) sugar
2 x 15ml sp (2tbsp) white wine vinegar
2 x 15ml sp (2tbsp) cooked or canned sweetcorn kernels
1 x 1.25ml sp (¼tsp) finely chopped habanero chilli or other type of chilli
100ml (3½fl oz) water
1 x 1.25ml (¼tsp) yellow mustard seeds
pinch of ground turmeric
1 x 5ml sp (1tsp) cornflour, blended with a little cold water
50g (1¾oz) papaya, cut into 5-mm (¼-inch) cubes

for seasoning mix
1 x 1.25ml sp (¼tsp) paprika
1 x 2.5ml sp (½tsp) onion powder
1 x 1.25ml sp (¼tsp) dried thyme
1 x 1.25ml sp (¼tsp) dried oregano
1 x 1.25ml sp (¼tsp) cayenne pepper
1 x 1.25ml sp (¼tsp) ground black pepper
1 x 2.5ml sp (½tsp) cornflour

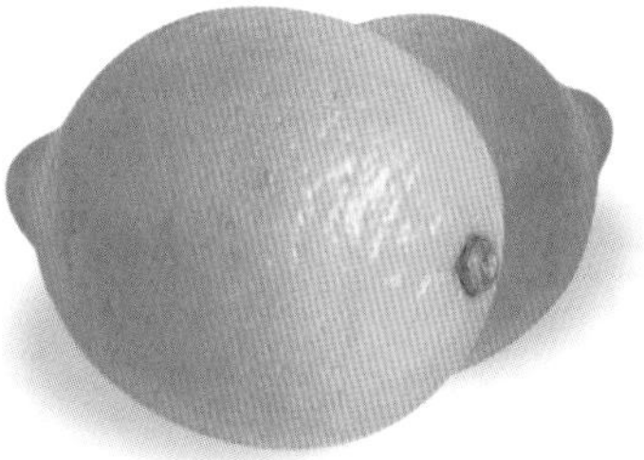

1. To make the relish, place the onion, sugar, vinegar, sweetcorn, chilli, water, mustard seeds and turmeric into a small saucepan over a medium heat and bring to the boil. Simmer for 10 minutes, then add the cornflour mixture, stirring constantly, and cook until it is the required consistency (it will thicken slightly when cooled). Stir in the papaya and leave to cool.
2. To make the seasoning mix, put all the ingredients into a small bowl and mix thoroughly.
3. Sprinkle the seasoning mix over the snapper fillets on both sides and pat into the flesh, then shake off any excess. Lay the fillets on a board.
4. Heat a non-stick frying pan over a high heat until smoking. Lightly spray both sides of the fillets with oil, then put into the hot pan and cook for 2 minutes. Turn the fillets and cook all the way through. (If the fillets are thick, finish the cooking under a preheated grill as the less intense heat will prevent the seasoning mix from burning.) Remove the fish from the pan.
5. Add the lemon halves, cut-side down, and cook over a high heat for 2–5 minutes until browned. Serve the fillets, topped with relish, on warmed plates, with the lemon halves.

NUTRITION INFORMATION
per serving

calories	fat	sat fat	salt
100	2g	0.3g	0.2g

3% FAT | 140 CALORIES | SALT BALANCED

Salmon and prawn spring rolls with plum sauce

prep 30 minutes + 45 minutes cooling | **cook** 25 minutes | **serves** 4

125g (4½oz) salmon fillet, skinned, boned and cut into 3-mm (⅛-inch) cubes
60g (2¼oz) beansprouts
60g (2¼oz) Chinese leaf, finely shredded
25g (1oz) spring onion, finely chopped
60g (2¼oz) deseeded red pepper, finely sliced into strips
1 x 1.25ml sp (¼tsp) five-spice powder
60g (2¼oz) peeled, cooked prawns
4 spring roll wrappers, halved widthways
vegetable oil spray
1 x 1.25ml sp (¼tsp) sesame seeds

for the plum sauce
100ml (3½fl oz) water
50ml (2fl oz) freshly squeezed orange juice
1 x 2.5ml sp (½tsp) chopped red chilli
1 x 5ml sp (1tsp) grated root ginger
200g (7oz), stoned weight, red plums
1 x 5ml sp (1tsp) chopped spring onion
1 x 5ml sp (1tsp) chopped fresh coriander leaves
1 x 1.25ml sp (¼tsp) sesame oil

1. Preheat the oven to 180°C/350°F/Gas Mark 4.
2. To make the sauce, put the water, orange juice, chilli, ginger and plums into a medium, lidded saucepan and bring to the boil. Reduce the heat, cover and simmer for 10 minutes. Remove from the heat, blend with a hand-held electric blender, or use a food processor, then stir in the spring onion, coriander and sesame oil. Leave to cool.
3. Heat a non-stick wok over a high heat, add the salmon and stir-fry for 1 minute. Remove from the wok with a slotted spoon onto a plate. Using the cooking juices from the salmon, stir-fry the vegetables with the five-spice powder until just tender, drain in a colander, then stir in the cooked salmon and prawns – the mixture should be quite dry to prevent the pastry from becoming soggy.
4. Divide the salmon and vegetable mixture into 8 portions. Spoon each portion along one short edge of each pastry rectangle and roll up, tucking in the sides.
5. Lay the spring rolls on a non-stick baking tray and spray lightly with vegetable oil, sprinkle with sesame seeds and bake in the oven for 12–15 minutes, or until golden brown.
6. Serve the spring rolls with the cold plum sauce separately.

NUTRITION INFORMATION
per serving

calories	fat	sat fat	salt
140	5g	1g	0.7g

Vegetarian food can be both flavoursome and healthy, but in many respects a little more thought and planning is required in its preparation, since it often relies too heavily on high-fat foods such as dairy products and nuts, which although very nutritious contain high levels of fat.

Vegetarian mair

The same nutritional principles apply to a vegetarian diet as to a non-vegetarian diet – eat a wide variety of foods including lots of cereals, vegetables, fruit and moderate amounts of protein. And don’t forget that vegetarian food is not only for vegetarians – carnivores can also enjoy its considerable culinary delights.

courses

2.5% FAT | 113 CALORIES | SALT BALANCED

Spiced risotto cakes with mango, lime and cream cheese

V | prep 30 minutes + 30 minutes cooling | cook 45–50 minutes | serves 3

85g (3oz), peeled weight, onion, finely chopped
85g (3oz) leek, finely chopped
25g (1oz) arborio or other risotto rice
500ml (18fl oz) vegetable stock
85g (3oz) grated courgette
15g (½oz) fresh basil, chopped
25g (1oz) fresh wholemeal breadcrumbs
vegetable oil spray

for the filling
50g (1¾oz) 4% fat cream cheese
50g (1¾oz), peeled weight, mango, diced
1 x 5ml sp (1tsp) finely grated lime zest
1 x 5ml sp (1tsp) lime juice
pinch of cayenne pepper

1. Preheat the oven to 200°C/400°F/Gas Mark 6.
2. Heat a large, non-stick saucepan over a high heat, add the onion and leek and cook, stirring constantly, for 2–3 minutes, or until softened but not coloured.
3. Add the rice and stock, bring to the boil, then continue to boil, stirring constantly, for 2 minutes. Reduce the heat and cook for a further 15 minutes, stirring every 2–3 minutes.
4. When the rice is nearly cooked and has absorbed all the stock, stir in the courgette and basil and cook, continuing to stir, over a high heat for a further 5–10 minutes or until the mixture is sticky and dry. Turn out onto a plate and leave to cool.
5. Meanwhile, to make the filling, mix the cream cheese, mango, lime zest and juice and cayenne together in a bowl.
6. Divide the cooled rice mixture into 3 and form into cakes. Make an indentation in the centre of each cake and fill with 1 x 15ml sp (1tbsp) of the filling. Mould the sides up and over to seal in the filling, then reshape with a palette knife. Coat each cake with breadcrumbs and arrange on a non-stick baking tray.
7. Spray each cake lightly with oil and bake in the oven for 15–20 minutes, or until a light golden-brown colour. Serve with green leaf salad.

COOK'S TIP

• *It is important to use a really starchy rice like arborio or other risotto rice so that the cakes hold together during reheating. Stirring the rice breaks down the starch and helps with the moulding.*

NUTRITION INFORMATION

per serving

calories	fat	sat fat	salt
113	2.5g	0.8g	0.9g

1% FAT | 210 CALORIES | SALT BALANCED

Lentil bolognaise

V | prep 25 minutes | cook 20–25 minutes | serves 4

1 x 5ml sp (1tsp) rapeseed or vegetable oil
1 x 5ml sp (1tsp) crushed garlic
25g (1oz), peeled weight, onion, finely chopped
25g (1oz) leek, finely chopped
25g (1oz) celery, finely chopped
25g (1oz) deseeded green pepper, finely chopped
25g (1oz), peeled weight, carrot, finely chopped
25g (1oz) courgette, finely chopped
85g (3oz) flat mushrooms, diced
4 x 15ml sp (4tbsp) red wine
pinch of dried thyme
400g (14oz) canned tomatoes, chopped, strained through a colander, and the juice and pulp reserved separately
4 x 15ml sp (4tbsp) dried Puy lentils, cooked (see COOK'S TIP)
freshly ground black pepper, to taste
2 x 5ml sp (2tsp) lemon juice
1 x 5ml sp (1tsp) sugar
3 x 15ml sp (3tbsp) chopped fresh basil, plus extra sprigs to garnish
140g (5oz), uncooked weight, spaghetti

1. Heat a saucepan over a low heat, add the oil and garlic and cook, stirring, until golden brown. Add all the vegetables, except the mushrooms, increase the heat to medium and cook, stirring occasionally, for 10–12 minutes, or until softened and there is no liquid from the vegetables left in the pan. Add the mushrooms.
2. Increase the heat to high, add the wine and cook for 2 minutes. Add the thyme and juice from the tomatoes and cook until reduced by half.
3. Add the lentils and pepper, stir in the tomatoes and cook for a further 3–4 minutes.
4. Remove the pan from the heat and stir in the lemon juice, sugar and basil.
5. Serve the sauce with the cooked spaghetti, garnished with basil sprigs.

COOK'S TIP

- *Puy lentils can be cooked without presoaking. Rinse thoroughly, cover in fresh cold water and cook for 25–30 minutes, or until just tender.*

NUTRITION INFORMATION

per serving

calories	fat	sat fat	salt
210	2g	0.2g	0.02g

0.5% FAT | 235 CALORIES | SALT BALANCED

Thai yellow vegetable curry with brown basmati rice

V | prep 35 minutes | cook 25 minutes | serves 4

50g (1¾oz) deseeded yellow pepper, cut into 1-cm (½-inch) squares
50g (1¾oz) celery, cut into 5-mm (¼-inch) lengths
50g (1¾oz) baby corn cobs, cut into 5-mm (¼-inch) lengths
85g (3oz) leek, cut into 5-mm (¼-inch) lengths
100g (3½oz), peeled weight, sweet potato, cut into 1-cm (½-inch) cubes
300ml (½pint) pineapple juice
200ml (7fl oz) water
100g (3½oz) pak choi, shredded
50g (1¾oz) courgette, cut into 5-mm (¼-inch) cubes
50g (1¾oz) mangetout, thinly sliced into strips
3 x 15ml sp (3tbsp) lime juice
2 x 15ml sp (2tbsp) cornflour, blended with a little cold water
4 x 15ml sp (4 tbsp) low-fat natural yoghurt
4 x 15ml sp (4tbsp) chopped fresh coriander leaves
150g (5½oz) cooked brown basmati rice

for the spice mix
1 x 5ml sp (1tsp) finely chopped garlic
1 x 1.25ml sp (¼tsp) ground turmeric
1 x 5ml sp (1tsp) ground coriander
1 x 5ml sp (1tsp) finely chopped lemon grass
3 kaffir lime leaves
1 x 5ml sp (1tsp) finely chopped green chilli

1. To make the spice mix, pound all the spices to a fine paste using a pestle in a mortar.
2. Put the pepper, celery, baby corn cobs, leek, sweet potato, pineapple juice, water and the spice mix into a large, lidded saucepan and bring to the boil. Reduce the heat and skim the scum from the surface with a metal spoon. Cover and simmer for 15 minutes.
3. Add the pak choi, courgette and mangetout and cook for 2 minutes.
4. Add the lime juice, then gradually add the cornflour mixture, stirring constantly, and cook until thickened to the required consistency.
5. Remove the curry from the heat and leave to cool for 2–3 minutes. Stir in the yoghurt. (Do not boil once the yoghurt has been added or the curry will separate.)
6. Stir in the fresh coriander and serve the curry with the rice, garnished with a little extra fresh coriander.

NUTRITION INFORMATION

per serving

calories	fat	sat fat	salt
235	1g	0.2g	0.5g

1% FAT | 255 CALORIES | SALT BALANCED

Tofu moussaka

V | prep 30 minutes | cook 1 hour 30–35 minutes | serves 4

2 x 75g (2 x 2¾oz) baking potatoes, scrubbed
4 x 15ml sp (4tbsp) lemon juice
1 x 5ml sp (1tsp) rapeseed or vegetable oil
1 x 5ml sp (1tsp) sugar
2 x 5ml sp (2tsp) crushed garlic
1 x 5ml sp (1tsp) ground cumin
2 x 15ml sp (2tbsp) dried oregano
250g (9oz) aubergine, diced
100g (3½oz), peeled weight, onion, sliced
175g (6oz) deseeded mixed peppers, diced
200g (7oz) canned tomatoes, chopped
400ml (14fl oz) 0% fat natural yoghurt
2 x 15ml sp (2tbsp) cornflour
2 x 15ml sp (2tbsp) English mustard powder
200g (7oz) silken tofu, sliced
85g (3oz) beef tomato, cut into 3-mm (⅛-inch) slices

1. Preheat the oven to 190°C/375°F/Gas Mark 5.
2. Bake the potatoes in their skins in the oven for 45 minutes, then remove and cut into 3-mm (⅛-inch) slices.
3. Mix the lemon juice, oil, sugar, garlic, cumin and oregano together in a small bowl, then lightly brush over diced aubergine, reserving the remaining mixture. Spread out on a non-stick baking tray and bake in the oven for 15 minutes.
4. Heat the reserved lemon juice mixture in a small saucepan over a high heat, add the onion and peppers and cook, stirring occasionally, until lightly browned. Add the canned tomatoes, reduce the heat and simmer for 4 minutes.
5. In a separate saucepan, whisk the yoghurt and cornflour together, then bring to the boil, whisking constantly until the yoghurt boils and thickens (you must whisk constantly or the yoghurt will separate before thickening). When the yoghurt has thickened, remove from the heat and whisk in the mustard powder.
6. In an ovenproof dish, make as many separate layers of the ingredients as you can, with sauce in between, such as tofu, sauce, onion and peppers, sauce, aubergine, sauce, potato, sauce and tofu, then finish with a layer of beef tomato topped with sauce.
7. Bake in the oven for 20–25 minutes, or until golden brown on top.

NUTRITION INFORMATION

per serving

calories	fat	sat fat	salt
255	5.5g	1g	0.3g

1% FAT | 200 CALORIES | SALT BALANCED

Rustic roasted ratatouille and potato wedges with smoked paprika and fromage frais

V | prep 30 minutes | cook 1 hour | serves 4

300g (10½oz) potatoes in their skins, scrubbed
200g (7oz) aubergine, cut into 1-cm (½-inch) wedges
125g (4½oz), peeled weight, red onion cut into 5-mm (¼-inch) rings
200g (7oz) deseeded mixed peppers, sliced into 1-cm (½-inch) strips
175g (6oz) courgettes, cut in half lengthways, then into 1-cm (½-inch) slices
125g (4½oz) cherry tomatoes
90g (3¼oz) 0% fat fromage frais
1 x 5ml sp (1tsp) runny honey
pinch of smoked paprika
1 x 5ml sp (1tsp) chopped fresh parsley

for the marinade
1 x 5ml sp (1tsp) rapeseed or vegetable oil
1 x 15ml sp (1tbsp) lemon juice
4 x 15ml sp (4tbsp) white wine
1 x 5ml sp (1tsp) sugar
2 x 15ml sp (2tbsp) chopped fresh basil
1 x 5ml sp (1tsp) finely chopped fresh rosemary
1 x 15ml sp (1tbsp) finely chopped fresh lemon thyme
1 x 1.25ml sp (¼tsp) smoked paprika

1. Preheat the oven to 200°C/400°F/Gas Mark 6.
2. Bake the potatoes in their skins in the oven for 30 minutes, remove and cut into wedges – the flesh should not be completely cooked.
3. To make the marinade, put all the ingredients in a bowl and blend together with a hand-held electric blender until smooth, or use a food processor.
4. Put the potato wedges into a large bowl with the aubergine, onion, peppers and courgettes, pour over the marinade and mix thoroughly.
5. Arrange the vegetables on a non-stick baking tray and roast in the oven, turning occasionally, for 25–30 minutes, or until golden brown and tender. Add the tomatoes for the last 5 minutes of the cooking time just to split the skins and warm slightly.
6. Mix the fromage frais, honey and paprika together in a bowl.
7. Serve the vegetables with a little of the fromage frais mixture, and sprinkled with chopped parsley.

NUTRITION INFORMATION

per serving

calories	fat	sat fat	salt
200	3g	1g	0.06g

1% FAT | 121 CALORIES | SALT BALANCED

Roasted squash wedges with three-grain risotto, marjoram and asparagus

V | prep 20 minutes | cook 25 minutes | serves 4

1 x 200g (7oz) acorn squash or other type of squash, peeled, deseeded and cut into 4 wedges
1 x 5ml sp (1tsp) rapeseed or vegetable oil
100g (3½oz), peeled weight, onion, finely chopped
1 x 5ml sp (1tsp) crushed garlic
70g (2½oz) three-grain risotto mix (baldo rice, spelt and pearl barley – this is available ready-mixed)
600ml (1pint) vegetable stock
235g (8¼oz) asparagus tips
2 x 15ml sp (2tbsp) finely chopped fresh marjoram, plus extra to garnish
3 x 15ml sp (3tbsp) 0% fat fromage frais
2 x 15ml sp (2tbsp) finely chopped fresh parsley
freshly ground black pepper, to taste

1. Preheat the oven to 200°C/400°F/Gas Mark 6. Spread out the squash wedges on a non-stick baking tray and roast in the oven for 20 minutes, or until tender and golden brown.
2. Meanwhile, heat the oil in a medium saucepan over a high heat, add the onion and garlic and cook, stirring, until softened but not coloured. Add the risotto mix and stir in half the stock. Simmer, stirring occasionally, until the stock has reduced in the pan. Pour in the remaining stock and continue to cook, stirring occasionally, until the grains are tender.
3. Cut 175g/6 oz of the asparagus into 10-cm (4-inch) lengths and blanch in a saucepan of boiling water for 2 minutes. Drain and keep warm. Cut the remaining asparagus into 5-mm (¼-inch) slices and add to the risotto for the last 3 minutes of the cooking time.
4. Remove the risotto from the heat and stir in the marjoram, fromage frais and parsley. Season with pepper. Do not reboil.
5. To serve, lay the squash wedges on warmed serving plates, then spoon over the risotto and top with the asparagus. Garnish with marjoram.

COOK'S TIP

• *The three-grain risotto mix is available from most quality food shops and is ready-prepared, so it needs no presoaking or precooking. If you cannot readily find it, substitute 35g (1¼oz) risotto rice and 35g (1¼oz) pearl barley, precooked for 20 minutes.*

NUTRITION INFORMATION

per serving

calories	fat	sat fat	salt
121	1.5g	0.2g	0.2g

For years we have relied on a pan of boiling salted water to cook our vegetables. This not only has a detrimental effect on the nutritional content of vegetables but it is also the way to turn wonderful fresh

Vegetables and

vegetables into brown unappetising accompaniments. Roasting, chargrilling and braising are just three of the different methods of cooking vegetables and will enhance the natural flavours within the vegetables. For instance, next time you cook carrots, don't boil them in water, which only serves to leach all the flavour and the nutrients out of the carrots into the water; instead try roasting them in the oven. This way will remind you of how carrots used to taste.

The general rules are to buy fresh, cook less and be brave with your combinations and always remember that the flavourings used within the vegetable or side dish should complement, and not confuse, whatever you serve it with.

side dishes

3% FAT | 61 CALORIES | SALT BALANCED

Curly kale with sesame, ginger and spring onions

V | prep 10 minutes | cook 15 minutes | serves 2

150g (5½oz) curly kale
1 x 5ml sp (1tsp) sesame seeds, plus extra for sprinkling
1 x 5ml sp (1tsp) sugar
1 x 15ml sp (1tbsp) peeled and finely sliced root ginger
3 x 15ml sp (3tbsp) water
1 x 15ml sp (1tbsp) lemon juice
50g (1¾oz) spring onion, finely sliced
1 x 1.25ml sp (¼tsp) sesame oil

1. Remove all the thick stems from the curly kale. Bring a large, lidded saucepan of water to the boil. Add the kale, cover and cook for 6–7 minutes, or until tender. Drain in a colander and keep warm.
2. Heat a small saucepan over a high heat, add the sesame seeds and cook, tossing the pan, until golden brown.
3. Add the sugar, ginger, water and lemon juice. Cook until reduced by half, then add the spring onion and oil and simmer for 1 minute.
4. In a large bowl, toss the kale with the sesame seed sauce so that the leaves are well coated.
5. Serve on warmed plates with a few extra sesame seeds sprinkled over the top.

COOK'S TIP

• *This recipe can also be used with other green leaves, broccoli and French beans. Just blanch and toss in the sesame sauce.*

NUTRITION INFORMATION

per serving

calories	fat	sat fat	salt
61	3.5g	0.5g	0.08g

1% FAT | 49 CALORIES | SALT BALANCED

Roasted beetroot and shallots with thyme

V | prep 10 minutes | cook 25 minutes | serves 4

150g (5½oz), peeled weight, shallots, left whole
5g (⅛oz) sprigs of thyme, plus extra to garnish
2 bay leaves
200ml (7fl oz) water
freshly ground black pepper, to taste
250g (9oz) cooked beetroot, cut into 3-cm (1¼-inch) wedges
rapeseed or vegetable oil spray

1. Preheat the oven to 220°C/425°F/Gas Mark 7.
2. Put the shallots, thyme, bay leaves, water and pepper into a medium saucepan and bring to the boil over a high heat. Cook until the liquid is reduced and the sugar in the shallots has made it lightly syrupy.
3. Add the beetroot and stir to coat in the syrup. Transfer to a non-stick baking tray.
4. Spray the shallots and beetroot lightly with the oil and roast in the oven for 20 minutes, turning halfway through, until caramelised.
5. Serve in a warmed serving dish, garnished with thyme sprigs.

COOK'S TIP

• *Try this recipe with fresh rosemary instead of the thyme and serve with your favourite lamb dish.*

NUTRITION INFORMATION

per serving

calories	fat	sat fat	salt
49	1g	0.1g	0.2g

1% FAT | 58 CALORIES | SALT BALANCED

Spring greens, serrano ham and Jerusalem artichokes

prep 20 minutes | cook 15–20 minutes | serves 4

100g (3½oz) Jerusalem artichokes, peeled and cut into 2-cm (¾-inch) cubes
2 x 15ml sp (2tbsp) lemon juice
200g (7oz) spring greens, shredded
25g (1oz) serrano ham, thinly sliced into strips
1 x 5ml sp (1tsp) thinly sliced garlic
zest of 1 small lemon, cut into long, thin strips with a potato peeler
1 x 5ml sp (1tsp) sugar
freshly ground black pepper, to taste

1. Put the Jerusalem artichokes into a small saucepan, just cover with water and add 1tbsp of the lemon juice. Bring to the boil and cook for 3 minutes. Drain.
2. Bring a large saucepan of water to the boil, add the spring greens and cook for 3–4 minutes, or until just tender – do not overcook. Drain.
3. Heat a separate saucepan over a high heat, add the ham, garlic and lemon zest and stir-fry until golden brown. Stir in the sugar and remaining lemon juice, then add the artichokes and cook for 2–3 minutes. Season with pepper. Remove from the heat and keep warm.
4. Toss the artichoke mixture with the spring greens and serve on a warmed serving plate.

COOK'S TIP

- *Use presliced serrano ham in packs and remove all visible fat from the ham before cooking.*

NUTRITION INFORMATION

per serving

calories	fat	sat fat	salt
58	1g	0.3g	0.06g

0.6% FAT | 40 CALORIES | SALT BALANCED

Chargrilled fennel with orange and tarragon

V | prep 15 minutes | cook 30 minutes | serves 4

1litre (1¾pints) water
600g (1lb 5oz) fennel, quartered
4 bay leaves
1 x 5ml sp (1tsp) grated orange zest
100ml (3½fl oz) orange juice
1 x 5ml sp (1tsp) fennel seeds
1 x 15ml sp (1tbsp) chopped fresh tarragon
1 x 5ml sp (1tsp) cornflour, blended with a little cold water
rapeseed or vegetable oil spray
1 x 125g (4½oz) orange, peeled and quartered

1. Bring the water to the boil in a large, lidded saucepan and add the fennel and bay leaves. Reduce the heat, cover and simmer for 20 minutes, or until the fennel is tender. Drain in a colander, discarding the bay leaves, and keep warm.
2. Meanwhile, put the orange zest and juice, fennel seeds and tarragon into a small saucepan over a high heat and bring to the boil. Gradually add the cornflour mixture, stirring constantly, and cook until thickened. Remove from the heat, cover with clingfilm to prevent a skin forming and keep warm.
3. Heat a griddle pan over a high heat and spray lightly with oil. Add the fennel and cook, turning frequently, until golden brown on all sides.
4. Add the orange quarters and brown on both sides.
5. Serve the fennel and orange quarters with the sauce spooned over.

NUTRITION INFORMATION

per serving

calories	fat	sat fat	salt
40	0.5g	0.3g	0.06g

1% FAT | 33 CALORIES | SALT BALANCED

Roasted carrots with coriander, cumin and chilli

V | prep 15 minutes | cook 20–25 minutes | serves 4

300g (10½oz) carrots
1 x 15ml sp (1tbsp) coriander seeds
1 x 5ml sp (1tsp) cumin seeds
1 x 5ml sp (1tsp) finely chopped red chilli
1 x 15ml sp (1tbsp) lemon juice, plus extra to serve
1 x 5ml sp (1tsp) rapeseed or vegetable oil
2 x 15ml sp (2tbsp) chopped fresh coriander leaves, to garnish

1. Preheat the oven to 200°C/400°F/Gas Mark 6.
2. Peel and trim the carrots, then cut in half lengthways if they are small or into quarters if large.
3. Pound the coriander and cumin seeds in a mortar with a pestle, then blend in the chilli, lemon juice and oil.
4. In a large bowl, toss the carrots with the spice mix, then spread out on a non-stick baking tray and roast in the oven for 20–25 minutes, or until tender and golden brown.
5. Serve the carrots on a warmed plate with a good squeeze of lemon juice, garnished with fresh coriander.

COOK'S TIP

- *This recipe works well with pumpkin and squash.*

NUTRITION INFORMATION

per serving

calories	fat	sat fat	salt
33	1g	0.2g	0.04g

0.5% FAT | 91 CALORIES | SALT BALANCED

Braised lentils with root vegetables, vinegar and honey

V | prep 20 minutes | cook 20–25 minutes | serves 4

50g (1¾oz), peeled weight, onion, diced
50g (1¾oz), peeled weight, carrot, diced
50g (1¾oz) celery, diced
50g (1¾oz), peeled weight, turnip, diced
50g (1¾oz) leek, diced
2 x 15ml sp (2tbsp) chopped fresh thyme
2 bay leaves
85g (3oz) dried Puy lentils
600ml (1pint) vegetable stock
2 x 15ml sp (2tbsp) mature sherry vinegar
1 x 15ml sp (1tbsp) runny honey
freshly ground black pepper

1. Heat a medium, lidded saucepan over a high heat, add the vegetables and cook for 2–3 minutes, stirring constantly, until golden brown.
2. Add the thyme, bay leaves, lentils and stock and bring to the boil. Reduce the heat, cover and simmer for 15–20 minutes, or until the lentils are tender and have absorbed most of the stock.
3. Remove from the heat and stir in the vinegar and honey.
4. Serve on a warmed serving plate, with 1–2 grinds of black pepper.

COOK'S TIP

- *Serve these lentils with winter dishes such as casseroles, roasts and braises, or as a vegetarian main meal.*

NUTRITION INFORMATION

per serving

calories	fat	sat fat	salt
91	0.5g	0.1g	0.2g

Being on a diet should not be restrictive. In fact, it is extremely important to eat as varied and as interesting a diet as possible. And if you normally enjoy eating desserts, there is no need to deprive yourself of this little pleasure in life.

Desserts

A whole range of delicious desserts can be created using interesting fruits, filo pastry, low-fat fromage frais and yoghurt. We can't promise you a sticky toffee pudding but try these wonderfully light recipes, which will satisfy any sweet tooth and provide a grand finale to any meal.

0.5% FAT | 77 CALORIES | SALT BALANCED

Steamed spiced exotic fruits

V | prep 20 minutes | cook 10–12 minutes | serves 4

2 kiwi fruit, peeled and halved
4 rambutan or lychees, peeled, halved and stoned
2 passion fruit, the flesh scooped out
8 Cape gooseberries (physalis), papery leaves removed and fruit halved
85g (3oz), peeled weight, mango, cut into 2-cm (¾-inch) cubes
1 sharon fruit, cut into 2-cm (¾-inch) slices
85g (3oz) fresh raspberries
2 vanilla pods, split in half lengthways
2 cinnamon sticks, broken in half
4 star anise
4 fresh bay leaves
4 x 15ml sp (4tbsp) freshly squeezed orange juice

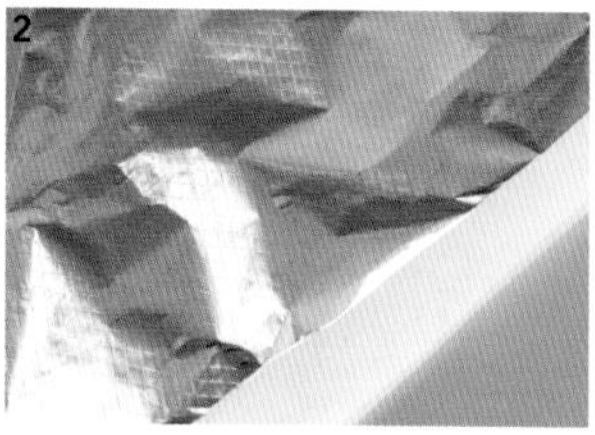

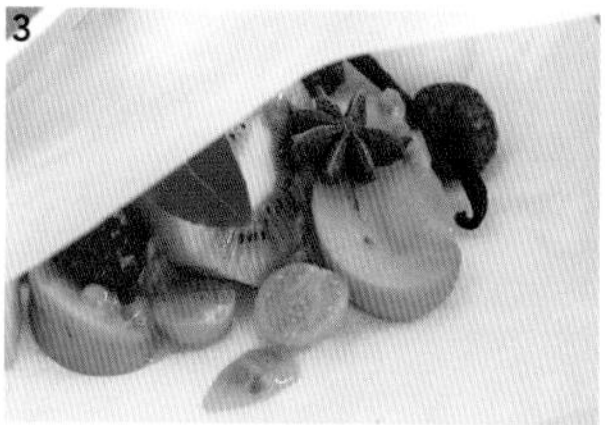

1. Preheat the oven to 200°C/400°F/Gas Mark 6.
2. Cut four 40 x 40-cm (16 x 16-inch) squares of baking paper and four foil squares of the same size. Put each baking paper square on top of a foil square and fold diagonally in half to form a triangle. Open up.
3. Divide the fruits into 4 and arrange each portion in the centre of each opened square – remember that you will be serving the fruit in the envelopes, so arrange the fruit neatly.
4. Add a vanilla pod half, a cinnamon stick half, a star anise, a bay leaf and 1tbsp orange juice to each triangle.
5. Close each triangle over the mixture, fold in the corners and crumple the edges together to form airtight triangular bags.
6. Transfer the bags to a baking tray and bake in the oven for 10–12 minutes, or until they puff up with steam.
7. To serve, put each bag on a serving plate and snip open at the table so that you can enjoy all the wonderful aromas as they are opened.

NUTRITION INFORMATION

per serving

calories	fat	sat fat	salt
77	0.5g	0.1g	0.002g

1% FAT | 100 CALORIES | SALT BALANCED

Banana and vanilla mousse cups

prep 20 minutes + 40 minutes chilling | **cook** 10 minutes | **serves** 4

200ml (7fl oz) semi-skimmed milk
1 vanilla pod, split in half lengthways
1 x 2.5ml sp (½tsp) vanilla extract
1 x 15ml (1tbsp) cornflour, blended with a little cold water
240g (8¾oz), peeled weight, banana, cut into 3-mm (⅛-inch) slices
1 x 15ml sp (1tbsp) caster sugar
2 x 15ml sp (2tbsp) water
1 gelatine leaf, soaked in cold water
2 medium egg whites

for the decoration
1 x 1.25ml sp (¼tsp) cocoa powder
4 fresh mint leaves

1. Pour the milk into a small saucepan and add the vanilla pod and extract. Bring to the boil. Gradually add the cornflour mixture, stirring constantly, and cook until thickened. Remove from the heat and allow to cool.
2. Divide a third of the banana slices between four 250-ml (9-fl oz) glasses or cups.
3. Remove the vanilla pod from the thickened milk and add the remaining banana slices. Using a hand-held electric blender, blend the mixture until smooth, or use a food processor.
4. Put the sugar and water into a separate small saucepan and bring to the boil. Boil for 1½ minutes, then remove from the heat and stir in the soaked gelatine leaf.
5. In a large, very clean bowl, whisk the egg whites until soft peaks form, then whisk in the gelatine mixture. Using a metal spoon, gently fold in the banana mixture, being careful not to knock out the air in the whisked egg whites.
6. Pour the mixture over the sliced banana in the glasses or cups and place in the fridge to set for about 40 minutes.
7. To serve, lightly dust with cocoa powder and decorate with mint.

COOK'S TIP
• *These cups can also be served lightly frozen on a hot summer's day. Just pop them into the freezer for 20–25 minutes before serving.*

NUTRITION INFORMATION
per serving

calories	fat	sat fat	salt
100	1g	0.6g	0.15g

1.5% FAT | 130 CALORIES | SALT BALANCED

Berry fruit cheesecake

prep 40 minutes + 1½ hours cooling/chilling | **cook** 15 minutes | **serves** 4

for the bases

15g (½oz) oats
10g (¼oz) sunflower seeds
1 x 15ml sp (1tbsp) dried mixed berries
2 x 15ml sp (2tbsp) freshly squeezed orange juice

for the filling

1 x 15ml sp (1tbsp) water
2 gelatine leaves, soaked in cold water
1 x 15ml sp (1tbsp) runny honey
250g (9oz) cottage cheese
100g (3½oz) 0% fat fromage frais
1 x 15ml sp (1tbsp) finely grated lemon zest
1 x 15ml sp (1tbsp) vanilla extract

for the topping

200g (7oz) frozen mixed summer fruits
1 x 5ml sp (1tsp) arrowroot, blended with a little cold water

1. Preheat the oven to 160°C/325°F/Gas Mark 3.
2. To make the bases, put all the ingredients into a food processor and process to a paste. Spread out on a non-stick baking tray and bake in the oven for 8 minutes. Remove, chop into 5-mm (1/4-inch) chunks, then return to the oven for a further 4–5 minutes, or until golden brown. Leave to cool, then process again. The mixture becomes crisp when cold.
3. Divide the mixture between 4 mini gateaux rings or ramekins, pressing it into the bases.
4. To make the filling, put the water, gelatine leaves and honey into a small saucepan over a low heat and heat until the gelatine has dissolved.
5. Put the cottage cheese, fromage frais, lemon zest and vanilla extract into a food processor and process for about 4–5 minutes, or until the mixture is really smooth and the zest has almost disappeared. Pour in the gelatine mixture – ensure that the cheese mixture is at room temperature before adding the gelatine, otherwise it will not set correctly.
6. Pour the filling over the top of the bases and chill in the fridge for 30 minutes, or until set.
7. To make the topping, put the frozen fruit into a small saucepan over a medium heat and bring to the boil. Gradually stir in the arrowroot mixture and cook, stirring constantly, until thickened. Leave to cool.
8. Add the topping to the cheesecakes. Using a small knife, carefully cut around the edge of each gateaux ring and tap out onto serving plates, or, if using ramekins, serve in the dishes.

NUTRITION INFORMATION

per serving

calories	fat	sat fat	salt
130	2.5g	0.7g	0.06g

2.5% FAT | 60 CALORIES | SALT BALANCED

Spiced baked goat's yoghurt with figs and maple syrup

V | prep 15 minutes | cook 15 minutes | serves 4

200ml (7fl oz) goat's yoghurt
1 x 1.25ml sp (¼tsp) ground mixed spice
1 x 5ml sp (1tsp) maple syrup
1 x 1.25ml sp (¼tsp) vanilla extract
15g (½oz) dried figs, very finely chopped
1 medium egg white

for the decoration
2 fresh figs, sliced
1 x 1.25ml sp (¼tsp) maple syrup
fresh mint leaves

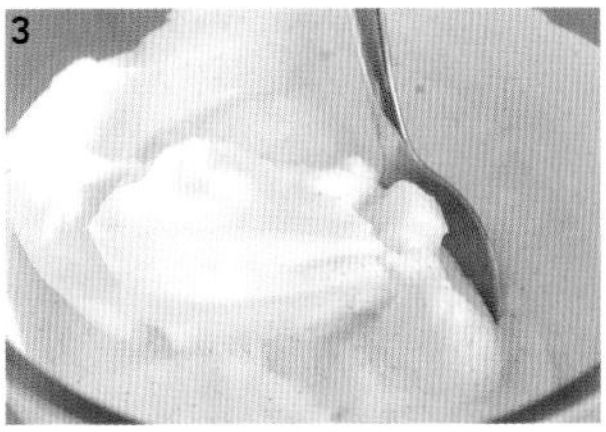

1. Preheat the oven to 140°C/275°F/Gas Mark 1.
2. Mix the yoghurt, mixed spice, maple syrup, vanilla extract and dried figs together in a large bowl.
3. In a separate, very clean bowl, lightly whisk the egg white until soft peaks form. Using a metal spoon, fold into the yoghurt mixture.
4. Spoon into 4 ramekins or a shallow, ovenproof dish.
5. Stand the ramekins or dish in a roasting tin and half-fill the tin with boiling water. Bake in the oven for 15 minutes or until set.
6. Remove from the oven. To serve, lay the fresh fig slices on top of the set yoghurts, drizzle with maple syrup and decorate with mint leaves.

COOK'S TIPS
- *These baked yoghurts can be served with other fruits such as peaches or pears when in season.*
- *The yoghurts can be served either hot or cold.*

NUTRITION INFORMATION
per serving

calories	fat	sat fat	salt
60	2g	1g	0.1g

1% FAT | 85 CALORIES | SALT BALANCED

Roasted English plums with honey, lavender, rosemary and redcurrants

V | prep 25 minutes | cook 20 minutes | serves 2

3 x 15ml sp (3tbsp) prune juice
2 x 15ml sp (2tbsp) freshly squeezed orange juice
4 strips of orange zest, cut with a potato peeler
1 sprig of rosemary
2 sprigs of lavender flowers, plus extra to decorate
1 x 5ml sp (1tsp) runny honey
25g (1oz) redcurrants
250g (9oz) ripe English plums, halved and stoned
3 x 15ml sp (3tbsp) 0% fat natural yoghurt, Greek style, to serve

1. Preheat the oven to 220°C/425°F/Gas Mark 7.
2. Put the prune juice, orange juice and zest, rosemary, lavender and honey into a small saucepan over a low heat and simmer for 4–5 minutes, until you have a light syrup. Remove from the heat, add the redcurrants and leave to cool.
3. Line a roasting tin with baking paper and arrange the plum halves in it, cut-side up. Spoon half the syrup over the plums, then roast in the oven for 15 minutes until soft. Remove from the oven.
4. Arrange the plums on a serving plate, spoon over the remaining syrup and top with the yoghurt. Decorate with lavender before serving.

COOK'S TIPS

- *This dish can be served hot or cold but is best served warm with chilled yoghurt.*
- *Choose only ripe plums for this dish so that the skins can be removed after roasting.*

NUTRITION INFORMATION

per serving

calories	fat	sat fat	salt
85	0.2g	0g	0.03g

0.5% FAT | 105 CALORIES | SALT BALANCED

Fresh raspberry and strawberry trifle

V | prep 20 minutes + 40 minutes cooling | cook 10 minutes | serves 2

1 x 5ml sp (1tsp) orange zest
85g (3oz) fresh strawberries
freshly ground black pepper, to taste
1 x 2.5ml sp (½tsp) arrowroot
1 x 5ml sp (1tsp) Cointreau
5 x 15ml sp (5tbsp) freshly squeezed orange juice
6 x 15ml sp (6tbsp) buttermilk
1 x 2.5ml sp (½tsp) vanilla extract
1 x 5ml sp (1tsp) sugar
15g (½oz) cooked meringue, broken into 5-mm (¼-inch) pieces
85g (3oz) fresh raspberries, plus extra to decorate
blanched strips of orange zest, to decorate

1. Mix the orange zest, strawberries and 1–2 grinds of black pepper together in a bowl.
2. Blend the arrowroot with the Cointreau. Put the orange juice into a small saucepan over a medium heat and bring to the boil. Gradually stir in the arrowroot mixture and cook, stirring constantly, until thickened. Remove from the heat, cover with clingfilm to prevent a skin forming and leave to cool completely.
3. Mix the buttermilk, vanilla extract and sugar together in a separate bowl.
4. Divide the strawberry mixture between 2 glasses, then pour over the thickened orange juice. Sprinkle the crumbled meringue on the strawberries, top with the raspberries and finally the vanilla buttermilk.
5. Decorate with a few extra raspberries and orange zest strips.

COOK'S TIP

- *These trifles are best arranged in the glass just before serving so that the meringue layer remains crunchy.*

NUTRITION INFORMATION

per serving

calories	fat	sat fat	salt
105	0.5g	0.2g	0.1g

1% FAT | 80 CALORIES | SALT BALANCED

Blueberry filo tart with lemon glaze

V | **prep** 20 minutes + 40 minutes cooling | **cook** 15 minutes | **serves** 2

4 sheets of filo pastry
rapeseed or vegetable oil spray
200g (7oz) 0% fat fromage frais
1 x 5ml sp (1tsp) honey
1 x 15ml sp (1tbsp) finely grated lemon zest
3 x 15ml sp (3tbsp) lemon juice
1 x 5ml sp (1tsp) caster sugar
100g (3½oz) fresh blueberries

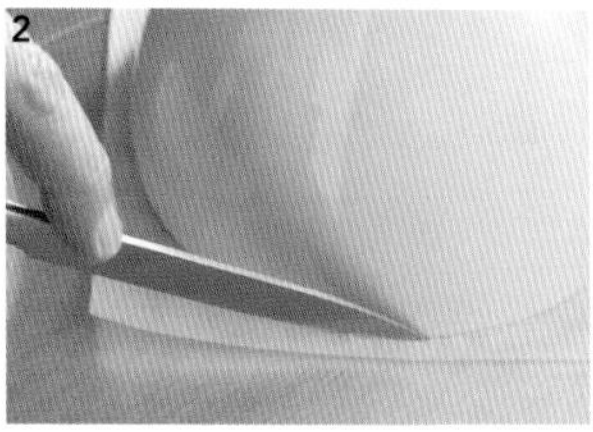

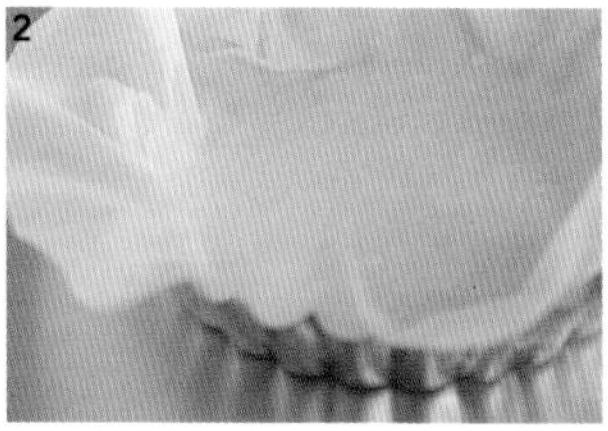

1. Preheat the oven to 180°C/350°F/Gas Mark 4.
2. Using a plate as a guide, cut out four 14-cm (5½-inch) circles of filo pastry (you need two circles per tartlet). Spray each lightly with oil before laying two circles into two 10-cm (4-inch) fluted tartlet tins, pressing the pastry into the corners. Prick the bases with a fork.
3. Put a ramekin into the centre of each tartlet case to prevent the pastry rising, then bake in the oven for 5 minutes. Remove the ramekins and bake the cases for a further 4–5 minutes so that the bases cook. Remove from the oven and leave the cases to cool in the tins. Store in an airtight tin so that they remain crisp.
4. Mix the fromage frais with the honey in a small bowl.
5. Put the lemon zest, juice and sugar in a small saucepan over a low heat and heat until the liquid has evaporated, then add the blueberries. Stir with a metal spoon to coat the berries in the syrup. Remove from the heat and keep warm.
6. To serve, place each tartlet case on a serving plate, spoon in a good dollop of the fromage frais mixture, then spoon over the warmed blueberries.

COOK'S TIPS

- *Make the tartlet cases in advance and keep for up to 3 days in an airtight container.*
- *The tartlets should be assembled just before serving so that the pastry does not become soggy.*

NUTRITION INFORMATION

per serving

calories	fat	sat fat	salt
80	0.7g	0g	0.04g

1.5% FAT | 85 CALORIES | SALT BALANCED

Really easy apricot and passion fruit sorbet with sesame snaps

V | prep 30 minutes + 2½ hours freezing | cook 25 minutes | serves 6

for the sorbet

100g (3½oz) ready-to-eat dried apricots
250ml (9fl oz) water
2 x 15ml sp (2tbsp) freshly squeezed lemon juice
2 x 15ml sp (2tbsp) freshly squeezed orange juice
7 x 15ml sp (7tbsp) passion fruit pulp, sieved to remove the seeds

for the sesame snaps (makes 16 snaps)

1 x 15ml sp (1tbsp) sesame seeds
1 x 15ml sp (1tbsp) liquid glucose
3 x 15ml sp (3tbsp) caster sugar
2 x 15ml sp (2tbsp) plain flour

1. To make the sorbet, put the apricots into a saucepan with the water and bring to the boil. Reduce the heat and simmer for 10–15 minutes, or until the apricots are soft. Remove from the heat.
2. Using a hand-held electric blender or a food processor, purée the apricots with the water, then blend in the lemon juice, orange juice and 3 x 15ml sp (3tbsp) of the passion fruit pulp.
3. Add 2 x 15ml sp (2tbsp) of the passion fruit pulp, mix well, then transfer to a large, freezer-proof container and freeze for 20 minutes.
4. Beat the sorbet to break down the ice crystals, then return to the freezer. Freeze for a further 2 hours 10 minutes, or until fully frozen, beating every 20 minutes to give a smooth texture to the finished sorbet.
5. To make the sesame snaps, preheat the oven to 180°C/350°F/Gas Mark 4.
6. Heat a small saucepan over a high heat, add the sesame seeds and cook, tossing the pan, until golden brown. Remove from the heat, add the glucose, sugar and flour and mix with a metal spoon to form a sticky paste. Remove from the pan and leave to cool slightly.
7. Roll the paste into a sausage shape and cut into 16 equal-sized pieces.
8. With wet hands, roll each piece into a small round ball (add a little room temperature water if the paste is too dry), then lightly press out onto a sheet of silicone and bake in the oven for 6 minutes until golden brown. Remove from the oven. Using a palette knife, remove from the silicone and leave to cool on a wire rack, then transfer to an airtight container.
9. Using an ice cream scoop, scoop the sorbet into glasses, spoon the remaining passion fruit pulp over the top and serve with 2 sesame snaps per serving.

NUTRITION INFORMATION

per serving

calories	fat	sat fat	salt
85	1.5g	0.2g	0.02g

Index